CREATING INSTRUCTIONAL SEQUENCES

CREATING INSTRUCTIONAL SEQUENCES

Ernest Siegel, EdD
Rita Siegel, MS Ed

ACADEMIC THERAPY PUBLICATIONS
NOVATO, CALIFORNIA 94947

Academic Therapy Publications
20 Commercial Boulevard
Novato, California 94947

Tests, books, and materials
for and about the learning disabled

Library of Congress Cataloging in Publication Data
Siegel, Ernest.
    Creating instructional sequences.

1. Lesson planning. I. Siegel, Rita, joint author.
II. Title.
LB1027.S49   371.3   77-11107
ISBN 0-87879-175-2
ISBN 0-87879-176-0 pbk.

This book was set in IBM Century 10 point
medium, italic, and bold type. The display type
was 36 point and 18 point Friz Quadrata. The
paper used was 60 pound White Book for the
text; 10 point CIS for the cover of the soft-
bound edition; Arrestox B for the cover of the
hardbound edition.

Preface

Since the advent of educational measurement about half a century ago, teachers have been given advice by other professionals. Unfortunately, the teachers more often have been intimidated by other professionals than helped by them. Ernest and Rita Siegel's book, however, bridges the gap between technicians and theorists, and addresses itself to the critical and detailed aspects of developing instructions to meet the needs of each individual child. Goals and objectives have been around for years. In the past few years, many educators have talked about performance criteria, desired outcomes and management by objectives. As a result, significant pressures have been brought on educators about specifying the proposed outcome of their product; however, little effort has been directed at how to get to the product. The Siegels bridge the gap between the process and the product by simply sequencing the skills necessary for creating instructional sequences—which is necessary for good teaching.

It is refreshing to read that teaching—teaching *effectively*—does not depend on membership in a society, or on the use of wide variety of materials or specific methods declared by categorical labels. Teaching, even teaching exceptional children, requires that one be aware of the entering behaviors of the learner, knowing the requirements necessary for the task's successful completion, and then developing instructional sequences to match the learning profile of the pupil. This book offers a refreshing approach to teaching and the authors write with authority, simple eloquence, and clarity. The guidelines on how to write instructional sequences are practical, clear, and easily readable. There is something here for the novice as well as for the astute veteran classroom teacher.

By delineating the critical skills necessary for the product, the authors have kept with the theme of their book. The book itself illustrates that they have imparted the knowledge or the skills necessary to write instructional sequences. They do not merely present, but teach: teach us to prepare, create, and evaluate instructional sequences.

The ideas and techniques set forth in this book were developed and listed in practical teaching situations which involved both children and teachers.

Ernest and Rita Siegel present no grand theory on the learning problems of children, nor do they advocate certain materials, nor do they claim to present a final word on any topic. Readers who review this book systematically will find herein a marvelously useful set of tools in finished form, and others in suggestions which teachers can adapt to create their own instructional sequences to improve their own teaching.

Creating Instructional Sequences is informative and challenging; I invite your thoughtful and reflective reading of the work with the hope that it will be as rewarding to you as it was for me.

Hubert "Booney" Vance, PhD
Director, Child Study Center
James Madison University
Harrisonburg, Virginia

Acknowledgments

We are indebted to the many professionals who encouraged us in this project and who gave us many valuable suggestions. These include our colleagues at Adelphi University: Professors David Levinsky, Ruth Gold, Joan Bildman, George Benner, and Sheldon Stoff.

We also appreciate the opportunity given us to present workshops, demonstrations, and inservice training devoted to instructional sequences. Among these are the special education departments in the University of New Mexico; Keene State College, New Hampshire; Appalachian State University, Boone; College of New Rochelle, New York; Adelphi University, Garden City, New York; State Department of Education, Dover, Delaware; Jefferson County Public Schools, Lakewood, Colorado; Rutgers University, New Jersey; West Georgia University, Carrolton, Georgia.

Mr. Al Harris, president of Educational Activities, Inc., Freeport, New York, graciously consented to our quoting a portion of a previously published book, *Teaching One Child.*

Finally, we are especially thankful to our many special education students for their ideas, suggestions, and interest.

Ernest Siegel
Rita Siegel

To all children—but especially to handicapped learners—who desperately cry out their needs, and to the dedicated teachers who listen.

Contents

Part Three: Perspectives

Introduction

Creating instructional sequences is the only way to teach! It is our contention that this statement is correct, granted two stipulations: (1) we are emphasizing the "imparting knowledge or a skill" theme of education, and (2) we are focusing upon handicapped learners. To state this another way, the handicapped learner has already shown that he cannot readily learn by himself, incidentally, tangentially. For him, mere presentation—instead of systematic, precise instruction—simply will not do.

All of the classic definitions of mental retardation—and therefore, reciprocally, of intelligence—include the criterion of adaptive behavior. How, indeed, does an intelligent being (that is, a nonhandicapped learner) adjust to a meager educational environment? He learns, anyhow. Steps can be out of order, instructional objectives ill-stated (the teacher may be unclear regarding the lesson's aim) or ill-chosen (the level may appear too difficult for the child in question), the "instruction" consisting solely of requiring the pupil to demonstrate abilities in that which has not yet been taught, educational strategies nil or illogical, and still the normal or gifted learner continues to learn. In fact, it is not at all a rare phenomenon to see children entering first grade already able to read and do arithmetic at the first- and second-grade level. All this, of course, is not to suggest that good learners do not need good teachers. Teaching them effectively is a special kind of challenge in that the instructor must provide enrichment and motivation, must deal with the higher complexity of subject matter, must nourish creativity, must take into account huge discrepancies between intellectual level and physical, social, and emotional maturity, and should proceed at a relatively rapid rate.

Imparting knowledge or skill is no picayune consideration. Think of all the times during the school day that teachers endeavor to do just that. They want to teach their pupils to multiply by five, to form plurals of nouns, to recognize phonic blends, to tell time, to tie their shoelaces, to use a wood plane, to solve simultaneous equations, to differentiate between simile and metaphor, to fold a piece of paper in half, to use a ruler correctly, to identify shapes, to conjugate a verb, to outline an essay, to write the letter *G*, to use the typewriter, to recognize synonyms and antonyms, to read the grid points on a map, to measure angles, to identify key signatures on musical staffs, to spell correctly, and so on, *ad infinitum*. The teacher should not be distracted or discouraged by this seemingly endless list of discrete skills. Rather, it should direct the teacher's efforts toward the need for good teaching: systematizing, structuring, sequencing.

Sequencing cuts across all grade levels and all subject areas. It facilitates growth of broad developmental processes: perception (including laterality, directionality, body image, spatial orientation, auditory and visual memory, etc.), coordination, language, and the cognitive process itself. It is instrumental in remediating psychoeducational deficits such as distractibility, disorganization, and anxiety. It is a vital aspect in the application of behavior modification techniques (i.e., shaping requires the systematic breaking down of the target behavior into a set of sequentialized subbehaviors).

Certainly, one is aware that education means more than shoveling knowledge and skills into children. Such considerations as maintaining rapport, developing creativity, fostering initiative, providing pleasurable experiences (e.g., "reading for enjoyment") are all important. So, imparting knowledge or a skill may not be the whole of education, but it is the heart of it. And when it comes to learning how to do this, the flow will always be from special education to general education, from teaching handicapped learners to teaching normal and gifted learners, from providing instructional intervention for those who absolutely require it to helping the nonhandicapped, relatively independent learner to learn even more.

To the extent that imparting knowledge or a skill is important, to that extent is the teacher's ability to create instructional sequences paramount. This book is the culmination of over a dozen years of teacher-training in which instructional sequences were considered, created, evaluated, and refined. Guidelines for writing them, yardsticks for evaluating them, and—above all—instructional techniques and strategies for designing them were developed.

There is much literature (articles, chapters, monographs, and at least one complete book*) which systematically and effectively presents instruction in formulating educational objectives. We consider this a milestone in education. If one is endeavoring to teach, then the question, "What do I want to teach?" certainly ought to be asked and answered. After answering that question correctly, the inquisitive and conscientious teacher must immediately ask another question, "How can I best teach it?"

Perhaps this work can provide some answers.

---

*Robert Mager, *Preparing Instructional Objectives* (Palo Alto, California: Fearon, 1962).

Part One: Orientation

CHAPTER ONE

Rationale

There are many cogent arguments which justify the emphasis upon instructional sequencing for handicapped learners. First, sequencing is a prime vehicle by which structure can be achieved. The literature is replete with pleas—and rationales—for providing structure in educating the learning and/or behaviorally impaired. The learning disabled (sometimes referred to as "minimally brain dysfunctioned") need it as an antidote to perceptual impairment: They are not able to focus readily upon significant sensory data, to receive these without distortion, or to organize them into meaningful wholes. The emotionally disturbed warrant it because it provides limits, boundaries, and rules, conveys a message that someone cares enough to set these limits (i.e., to establish clear, attainable, individualized educational goals), and sets the stage for improved self-concept since academic achievement becomes possible—often for the first time. The mentally retarded benefit by it in that any given skill can be broken down into subskills and each of these presented in frames sufficiently discrete to facilitate success; moreover, it nurtures attention in that the child is, at each step, required to *do* something.

Another reason for stressing instructional sequencing stems from the fact that recently the value of perceptual training as a highly publicized and important ingredient in special education has been questioned. Donald Hammill, in an article analyzing twenty-five studies (each addressing itself to the question of whether or not perceptual training boosts reading ability), came to a sobering conclusion: There is no evidence that reading ability is nourished by perceptual training.* A question immediately arises: If a

*Donald D. Hammill, "Training Visual Perceptual Processes," *Journal of Learning Disabilities* 5:9 (November 1972): 552-559.

given handicapped learner does not need perceptual training, then what *does* he need? Why, good teaching (namely, instructional sequencing), or course!

The current cry for teacher accountability provides yet another reason for instructional sequencing. If, indeed, teachers are to be held accountable for pupil failure, then fairness would dictate that they first be guided toward (1) viewing the individual child's entry level, (2) selecting an appropriate, discrete, definitive instructional aim, and (3) breaking the aim down into sequentialized steps—each one related to the objective, clear, precise, and a prerequisite to the next step. To pursue this point, educators are ill-advised to encourage teachers to be aware of the affective needs of pupils, to be ever-cognizant of the "whole child," even to make valid educational diagnoses, if we fail to show them how to *teach*.

It is ironic that "imparting knowledge or a skill" is the heart of education and, at the same time, is the only element that lends itself so handily to self-deception. Consider a few of the other elements of education. Routines: If routines are not maintained and disorganization is rampant, it is not likely that the teacher will claim that her lessons are well organized. Curriculum: If she is unfamiliar with the curriculum, the teacher will probably not profess that she is following it. Rapport: If her students express open hostility toward her, are negative, unwilling to cooperate or even to communicate with her, the teacher will not readily proclaim that positive rapport has been established. Modifications: If the teacher has not considered appropriate modifications for any given child, it would be virtually impossible for her to tell herself (or others) that her lessons are individualized and tailor-made for each child. And yet, the same teacher can quite easily delude herself regarding "imparting knowledge or a skill." You see, all the ingredients are there—the children, a classroom, materials, the teacher, and *some* activity—so why not call it *teaching*? Certainly, a sense of instructional sequencing can go a long way toward enabling the teacher to identify those times when teaching is indeed occurring.

There is overflow from the teacher's prowess as an imparter of knowledge or skills into the vital area of classroom management. Misbehavior can seldom be attacked directly, but it often can be worked through via effective teaching. The teacher who becomes proficient in creating and implementing instructional sequences cannot help but grow in self-confidence: "I really know how to sequence—that is *teach*!" This feeling of self-confidence, when coupled with a high degree of organization, considerable self-discipline, a strong sense of precision regarding the task's steps, and a sense of relevance regarding matching the requirements of the task to the learning weakness/strength profile of the child, and the overall ability to prepare well-developed lessons (all, by the way, nourished by the commitment to—and practice of—creating instructional sequences), manifoldly increases the teacher's ability in classroom management. In the middle of a lesson utilizing an appropriate, well-developed sequence, should a given child begin exhibiting poor impulse control, the teacher's pedagogical savoir-faire and self-assurance virtually exude: "Come on, Charles, we simply do not have time for that sort of behavior. I know just what you need to learn and exactly how to help you learn. Please let me help you." However, if the teacher is not teaching sequentially—that is, is imprecise, does not know specifically what she is

16

doing, and is, in general, unsure of herself—then the most minute outburst of misconduct can easily "throw her off." She will probably give it too much attention, thereby causing it to mushroom. After all, it is easy to get side-tracked from what one is doing if, in reality, one is doing nothing. Stated differently, if you are interrupted in the middle of "teaching," it is difficult to get back to where you were, in fact, noplace. Thus, we see that there is a strong relationship between the teacher as instructor and the teacher as classroom manager. (Incidentally, there is a similar relationship between the child as a learner and the child as a behavor: Clearly, the pupil who can gain approval and feelings of success through academic accomplishment hardly has the need to seek recognition through disruptive behavior.)

Finally, in our efforts to provide optimal education for the disadvantaged, we ought to train our spotlight upon the area of good teaching (in other words, sequencing) rather than upon other seemingly more dramatic considerations. Edmund Gordon, a psychologist, explains:

> There are many good reasons for improving the living conditions of the disadvantaged: there is certainly no good excuse not to do so. But a concern on the part of the school for changing poor conditions of life should not substitute for a primary concern with the improvement of the teaching-learning process.*

*The Six-Hour Retarded Child, a report on a conference on problems of education of children in the inner city, August 10-12, 1969, The President's Committee on Mental Retardation, Office of Education, U.S. Department of Health, Education, and Welfare.

CHAPTER TWO

Sample Sequences

These sample sequences are presented early in the book so that the reader can obtain a clearer picture of what is being discussed. In perusing them, notice that there is no mention at all of a particular child's (or class's) needs, interests, academic level, learning profile, or the like. In fact, the closest they come to actual children is to specify the entering behavior that *any* learner would have to possess in his repertoire when arriving upon that instructional scene.

Sooner or later, every master teacher must make a discovery—one which, at the outset, seems so simple. Yet, as the mind mulls it over, its profundity, logic, and, above all, its pragmatic value becomes evident. It is this: There is a crucial difference between learning to write instructional sequences for hypothetical pupils as opposed to designing instructional procedures functionally, that is, on-the-job, in response to the educational needs of actual pupils. In a real sense, the first is a prerequisite of the second, and affords one the opportunity to focus more completely upon the task itself.

When given a behavioral objective and asked to write an appropriate instructional sequence, it is not necessary to have a case history of the pupil (or a composite class profile). In fact, too much emphasis upon the child himself (albeit he is the end product of all of our educational efforts) may becloud the immediate issue of increasing teaching competency. All that is necessary in learning to design instructional sequences is to assume that (1) the pupil is ready to learn the objective (this includes academic as well as physical, neurological, emotional, and motivational readiness), but (2) he cannot learn it without precise and systematic instructional intervention. (In real life, of course, the teacher *must* know the entering behavior of the child—or class—and use this knowledge in making decisions regarding the very selection of the task, as well as such other factors as modification, modalities to be used, and strategies to nurture motivation. Even so, however, granted only that the behavioral objective is in consonance with "where the child is at," then the sequence itself might be all the support, structure, modification, and motivation that is required.)

Sample Sequence I: Using the "More Than" and "Less Than" Signs

Behavioral Objective

> When presented with an arithmetical "sentence" using signs, $<$ or $>$, the child will be able to read the "sentence" correctly; if the signs have been omitted, the child will be able to insert them, pointed in the proper direction, so as to make the "sentence" correct. (Numbers range from 1 to 10.)

Entering Behavior

> The child can recognize and write numerals 1 to 10, is beginning to develop an understanding of the concepts "more" and "less," and knows that reading proceeds from left to right.

Instructional Sequence

1. Discuss "more than" or "less than" using materials (e.g., two groups of pennies, two groups of blocks, etc.). Ask the child to point to the correct group.

   a. at first, make the difference large (e.g., 10 and 2).
   b. sometimes, synonyms help develop the child's concepts: "big bunch," "the most," "whole lot," "biggest pile," etc. (The superlative, though incorrect grammatically, serves to dramatize the differences in size to the child.) When deemed necessary, use these synonyms at this stage of the sequence.
   c. vary the order of the groups so that the largest does not always appear first.

2. The child places a cardboard cut-out shaped like the sign between two groups of objects. (This eliminates any distractions and digressions which could be caused by visual-motor problems if the child were asked to write the sign.)

   Cue:

   > The "mouth of the puppy" goes toward the biggest group of cookies.　　　　　　　　　　　　　*or*

   > The big part goes to the big group.
   > The small part goes to the small group.

   Try several pairs, placing the cutout between the two groups of objects. Keep the differences large. Continue to prompt with synonyms and the "puppy" cue. The child is instructed to read the "sentence" as well as to place the sign in appropriate position. (If necessary, remind him that reading progresses from left to right.)

3. This is the same as Step 2, but gradually decrease the differences and fade out use of synonyms, but keep the "puppy" cue. Continue to vary the order of the group.

4. Write the sign (< or >) between two groups of objects which have been placed on paper. (If the child has difficulty writing the sign, he may use the cutout's edge to help rule the lines; at any rate, success in Steps 2 and 3 makes it more likely that the child will write the sign correctly.) The child does several sets under the teacher's supervision. Continue to vary the order of the groups. The teacher reads aloud each "sentence" and asks child to do the same. (Remind him of left-right progression.)

5. Write the signs between two numbers. At first, the child works several sets under the teacher's supervision. Then he completes a worksheet independently, as shown in the following illustration

Fill in the correct sign: < or >	
2 < 8	6 > 5
4 < 7	8 < 10
10 1	3 0

6. Practice reading the "sentence" from left to right (e.g., "two is less than eight"; "six is more than five"). The child must read all sentences of his worksheet, as well as other individual ones which the teacher has prepared on index cards.

Sample Sequence II: Touching and Naming "Top" and "Bottom" of a Horizontal Plane

Behavioral Objective

When a blank sheet of 8½" by 11" paper is placed on the child's desk, the child (seated) will demonstrate his knowledge of "top" and "bottom" horizontally by, upon command, touching and naming the top and bottom of the paper.

Entering Behavior

The child already understands *up* and *down*, and *top* and *bottom* vertically.

Instructional Sequence

1. Instruct the child to stand and touch the top of the teacher and the bottom of the teacher.

2. While he is still standing, place a full-length picture (drawing) of a person in front of the teacher and instruct the child to touch the top and the bottom.

3. Show the child smaller pictures of the identical person, gradually reducing the dimensions to 8½" by 11" and instructing the child to touch the top and bottom of each.

4. Using a tiltboard on the child's desk, gradually rotate the picture to a horizontal position, instructing him to touch the top and the bottom at various intervals during the rotation.

5. Place the picture on the child's desk, and the child (seated) touches the top and the bottom of it.

6. Gradually fade out the picture by placing a succession of sheets of tracing paper over it; the child is instructed to touch the top and the bottom each time.

7. Replace these papers with a blank sheet of paper 8½" by 11". The child is instructed to name the top and bottom as the teacher points to them, and conversely, to touch them, upon command.

Sample Sequence III: Differentiating Between *S* and *SM* as Applied to Decoding

Behavioral Objectives

A. Given 20 words beginning with *s* or *sm*, the child will be able to identify the initial consonant sound or consonant blend with 90 percent accuracy.

B. Given 20 letter clusters (e.g., -ile, -ort, -ell) and told how each sounds, the child will be able to vocalize the whole word formed when *s* or *sm* is put before the cluster with 90 percent accuracy.

Entering Behavior

The child has demonstrated that he auditorially recognizes and can produce (vocalize) the sounds of all the consonants. (If the student who failed to learn the *s* and *sm* lesson did so because he did not know the individual consonant sounds, then no sequence written to teach the former is appropriate for him because he is not yet ready for it.)

Instructional Sequence

The teacher introduces a chart (or large paper on child's desk) showing the letters *s* and *sm* written in red. A sad face is posted under the *s*, and the word *sad* is written beneath the picture. The *s* in *sad* is also colored red.

A happy face is under the *sm* and the word *smile* (with *sm* in red)· written beneath it.

1. Review the sound of *s*

   a. The teacher makes the pure sound (*s* is not attached to any word) and asks the child to name the letter.

b. The teacher points to letter (on chart) and child is required to give its sound. (The foregoing is all part of prerequisite skills.)

2. Introduce the *sm* sound
   a. The teacher points to *sm* on the chart and makes the pure sound. She tells the child that this is how the *s* and the *m* sound when joined (or blended). She uses slow, exaggerated speech at first.
   b. The teacher makes pure *sm* sound (still fairly slowly) without pointing to chart and the child is required to name letters. (He may refer to the chart.)
   c. The teacher points to *sm* on chart and asks the child to produce the pure sound. (The child should be encouraged to hold sound of both *s* and *m* to reinforce auditory and kinesthetic cues.)

3. The child is required to differentiate between the pure *s* and *sm* sounds.
   a. The teacher makes one of the pure sounds, and the child is required to name the letter or letters she has sounded. She will shorten and lessen exaggerated speech as she proceeds. (Ten out of ten correct responses are required before next step is initiated.)
   b. The teacher points to either *s* or *sm*, and the child is required to produce the sound pointed to. The child will no longer be encouraged to exaggerate speech unless teacher detects sloppiness of reproduction. (Modification: Sometimes a child demonstrates that he cannot correctly reproduce the blended sound. He may put in extraneous sounds [e.g., "suh em"] or even produce an *sn* sound. At this point the sequence has to stop and a new sequence developed to teach the child how to blend.)

4. Add a nonsense syllable to the pure *s* and *sm* sounds. At this point, the cue chart is removed and replaced by a chart showing only the *s* and *sm*.
   a. The teacher explains that she will be adding the sound "ah" to the *s* and *sm*. She demonstrates how each will sound: "sah," "smah."
      — The teacher makes the sound, and the child tells which one he has heard (by pointing to it or, if it is labeled, by saying its number [e.g.: (1) sah, (2) smah]). The child must be able to correctly identify five out of five before the sequence proceeds.
      — The teacher points to the sound, and the child produces it. Five out of five correct responses are required. (It may

be at this point that the blending ability breaks down and a new sequence must be introduced.)

5. Introduce *s* and *sm* in actual words.

    a. The teacher vocalizes a word, and the child is asked to tell whether it begins with *s* or *sm*. If he can do this with 90 percent accuracy when given 20 different words, then the first behavioral objective has been achieved.

    b. A letter cluster is written on the board (or paper), and its sound is told to the child if he does not know it (e.g., -ell).

       — The teacher asks the child to tell what word it created when the *s* is put in front of the written *ell*.

       — The teacher continues this with 20 prepared letter clusters (or families) and varies the *s* and *sm* placed before them. The consonant or the blend plus the cluster must make a real word.

       — If the child can achieve 90 percent accuracy in this task, then the second behavioral objective has been achieved.

CHAPTER THREE

Guidelines

More and more, there is an evident need for greater precision in teaching. Both educators and practitioners readily agree that effective instruction begins when one matches the requirements of the task with the learning profile of the pupil. Despite the fact that there is no controversy in principle regarding the desirability of creating task-related instructional sequences, current classroom practices simply do not reflect this awareness.

It is likely that teachers would be more willing to embrace and to utilize the concept of instructional sequencing if specific guidelines for writing them could be drawn up.

Over the past several years, at various colleges, we have assigned to students (in special education as well as in regular education, both graduate and undergraduate students) a term paper requiring them to design instructional sequences for a variety of behavioral objectives. These included mastery in:

1. Multiplying by six.

2. Performing subtraction of two-digit numbers with exchange (regrouping).

3. Understanding and utilizing the alphabetizing system in preparation for alphabetizing 20 one-syllable word cards, each beginning with a different letter.

4. Distinguishing auditorially the long-*a* and short-*a* sounds, naming and producing either upon command.

5. Sawing a piece of wood.

6. Copying a paragraph of four sentences from the chalkboard.

7. Understanding the place-value system through number 99, identifying the numerical value of each digit as well as writing two-place numbers from dictation.

8. Identifying verbs, whether written or spoken.

On the basis of various cross-currents which ensued while designing these sequences, evaluating them, criticizing and refining them, certain guidelines have emerged:

Avoid Extraneous Material

It is not enough that activities within the sequence be related to its behavioral objective—they must be *directly* related to it. In teaching a pupil to multiply by six, it may be useful for the teacher to review the concept that the algorism "6 x 9" is really a symbol for six sets of nine objects. But to assign the pupil the laborious task of physically counting and arranging 54 squares of paper into representative sets is more a task of counting than it is of multiplying. The teacher who nevertheless deems it necessary for the pupil to actually *see* six nines would be astute if she prepares index cards with nine squares of paper already pasted on them.* The guiding slogan should be, "Let's get on with the task." Why destroy the tempo of the lesson and introduce tedious, nonessential, time-consuming activities? Similarly, wouldn't it be equally inane to order the pupil to copy twenty sentences from the chalkboard and underline every verb when the behavioral objective is simply to identify verbs?

It is, of course, possible to inject extraneous material unwittingly which is not even marginally related to the task. For example, one teacher who endeavored to instruct pupils to identify "action words" had them listen to a tape recording of various sounds (e.g., a phone's ring, a dog's bark, a bird's whistle). This was the very first step of the sequence, and the pupils, who were all handicapped learners, did not get the point. Perhaps if the teacher had asked the key question, "What is happening?" the pupils might have answered in verbs. She simply asked them, "What do you hear?" They responded, naturally, in nouns: phone, dog, bird. In retrospect, wouldn't it have been more basic to let the pupils watch someone (the teacher or a classmate) perform or pantomime some designated action? Isn't *seeing* action more germane than hearing it—especially since many actions do not produce sound?

In the sequence designed to teach the pupil to touch and name the "top" and "bottom" of an 8½" by 11" piece of paper horizontally (Sample Sequence II), it would have been totally irrelevant to ask him to consider the top *surface* and the bottom *surface* as being the "true" top and bottom.

---

*Of course, a good case could be made for entirely excluding this activity since it is definitely a prerequisite for the behavioral objective. That is, a handicapped learner who arrives at the stage where he is finally ready to learn the "six times table" should undoubtedly have grasped, at some earlier point, the *concept* of multiplying. Nevertheless, the teacher, endeavoring to be supportive, may plan to *review* this stage. Fine, but do it quickly!

Nor should he be told to rotate the horizontal paper from the North-South to the East-West axis and asked, *"Now* where is the 'top' and 'bottom'?" Unfortunately, one teacher even went so far as to include a step in which the pupil touches the top part of the paper v.ith his right hand and the top part of his head with his left hand simultaneously! Wouldn't all this have been confusing—and, what's more—patently unnecessary?

Likewise, some teachers, when asked to teach children to ride a two-wheeled bicycle, proposed having them begin by walking a straight line, walking on a balance board, or sitting on a wooden horse! Obviously, they are hung up on the word "balance." If this be the case, why not go all the way and ask the child to balance a basketball on his finger or a pointer on his nose? Clearly, the semantics of "balance" globally should not interfere with the teacher's concept as it specifically applies to bicycle riding.

At this point, the reader is urged to reexamine the three sample sequences. Notice that in each case, all steps are directly related to the stated behavioral objective. Do the same for each guideline. That is, after reading about a guideline, stop, review the sample sequences, and determine whether or not any step chosen purely at random reflects that guideline's principle.

Don't Spend Too Much Time in Reteaching the Prerequisite

If the aim of the sequence is to teach the child to multiply by six, then one must assume that the child already knows that multiplication is a short-cut to addition, the meaning of the multiplication sign, the commutative property of multiplication, and some of the prior "tables." If the child does not know all this and is in fact learning multiplication for the first time, then, why would the teacher want to begin with the sixes?

The "more than" and "less than" sequences (Sample Sequence I) starts at the review stage, but moves immediately (that is, in Step 2) to areas of instruction which are new to the pupil. Namely, he is introduced to the cardboard cutout ◀ , provided with a cue for determining the direction of placement, and instructed to make the actual placement. Similarly, the *s* and *sm* sequence (Sample Sequence III) *reviews* the *s* in Step 1, but introduces the new *sm* sound in Step 2. True, the second sample sequence ("top" and "bottom") *seems* to stay at the review stage (that is, the vertical plane) for the first three steps. This was necessary, however, since the pupil was being moved rapidly from a vertical person through a vertical life-size picture toward a much smaller vertical picture. Although the entering behavior proclaimed that the pupil already knew "top" and "bottom" from a vertical point of view, we had no right to assume that he knew it equally well for a small picture as for a large person. At any rate, there is no elaborate, time-consuming strategy in the first three steps (especially in Steps 1 and 2). As long as the hypothetical pupil has achieved the entering behavior to some extent regardless of the degree of mastery, these steps are deemed appropriate. At one extreme, they will serve as a quick review and will be over in two or three minutes. At the other extreme, some repetition will be necessary.

Similarly, if the aim is to teach the child the alphabetizing system so that he will be able to alphabetize twenty one-syllable word cards systematically, then one must assume that he already recognizes and can name all the letters. Remember, it was stipulated earlier that, for whatever instructional objective we wish to consider, our hypothetical pupil is ready to learn it. Hence, it would be ill-advised to devote too much energy in "teaching" him that which he already knows.

Of course, there is a relationship between the sequence's aim (i.e., the behavioral objective) and the teacher's knowledge of the child—his level, learning style, intact and impaired modalities, etc. Even a good sequence is useless if the child is not ready for it. Nevertheless, in practicing designing sequences, the teacher must decide what the prerequisites are, assure herself that somewhere there surely must be a child who has mastered these, and then get on with the job of writing the particular instructional sequence, starting at the point of the imaginary child's entering behavior.

Since the question of "to review or not to review" is two-sided, this guideline, "Don't spend too much time in reteaching the prerequisite," should be presented along with its corollary: "Use what the child knows to help him learn the new." It is all a question of degree. Although one should never unduly emphasize the reteaching of the prerequisite, review, per se, is not necessarily to be avoided. In fact, starting with what the child already knows renders support, is success-assuring, and is plainly sound pedagogy.

Most teachers probably teach the fives in multiplying before the sixes—not because five comes first but because finding the products is easier. They always end in zero or five. Moreover, because the fives are used in money, in telling time, scoring, etc., the teacher's instructional efforts are reinforced by these functional experiences. Therefore, a strategy for teaching multiplying by six might be to break up the six into five and one. Hence, 7 x 6 is approached by showing groups of seven nickels plus seven pennies. The child should already know both of these answers. He may, of course, need help in adding 35 + 7 mentally—but that, then, can be learned in a separate sequence.

This is not the only strategy for teaching multiplying by six in which optimal use of prerequisite skills is made. Let us assume that the pupil has already mastered prior multiplication tables—probably the ones, twos, threes, fours, fives, tens (these are easy and are often taught early) and maybe even the nines. (There is a trick to teaching this multiplication table. Both digits of the answer add up to 9 [e.g., in 7 x 9 = 63, the products 6 and 3 total 9]. The first digit is always one less than the "other number" [6 is one less than 7, the "other number"]. Many teachers show it to the child before most of the other tables are mastered in an effort to bolster ego and interest.) In addition, he should already know the commutative principle of multiplication. All that remains is to isolate those multiplication facts which he already knows: 1 x 6, 2 x 6, 3 x 6, 4 x 6, 5 x 6, 10 x 6, and possibly 9 x 6. Only three new facts remain: 6 x 6, 7 x 6, and 8 x 6 (or commutatively, 6 x 6, 6 x 7, 6 x 8); and these can be nurtured solely by memory: use of self-checking drill cards, repetitive writing of the algorism, repetitive saying of the algorism, visualization activities in which the algorism 6 x 7 = 42 is examined and studied for several seconds followed by a covering of the product, etc.

The entire area of developmental mathematics relies heavily upon number relationships. The astute teacher will strive to build the new upon that which the child already knows. Adding any one-place digit to nine can be facilitated by utilyzing the child's prior mastery of adding any one-place digit to ten (adding to ten is easier, isn't it?): when given 9 + 6, *think* of 9 + 1, then 10 + 5. Similarly, "near doubles" can be approached via "doubles": 6 + 7 can be taught by relating it to 6 + 6. (Experience has shown that "doubles" come easier.)

Assume Motivation

In the never-ending debate between humanism and behaviorism, some teachers seem compelled to devote a considerable portion of the sequence (often more than 50 percent of it) toward motivation.

One teacher proposed teaching a child to ride a bicycle by talking about transportation and visiting a bicycle store. Another began his sequence for teaching a child to saw a piece of wood by discussing carpentry and furniture, and then asking the child to choose one of five pieces of wood and one of five saws.

In the sequence designed to teach the pupil to differentiate the *s* from the *sm* blend (Sample Sequence III), a teacher proposed bringing in sugar, eggs, and an electric blender! The class agreed that, while this might have some benefit in motivating a particular child, the connection between this and the task itself is a tenuous one at best. It is likely that the teacher got sidetracked with the word "blend." After all, the behavioral objective was not for the child to develop an appreciation for the phenomenon of blending generally, but to be able to distinguish auditorially *sm* from *s*.

Notice that the "more than" or "less than" sequence (Sample Sequence I) did not require a trip to the circus to discover that there are fewer people in the classroom than at the circus. The "top" and "bottom" sequence (Sample Sequence II) did not necessitate a trip to the Empire State Building ("Look at the top!") or require the class to roll down hill ("Now you're at the bottom!"). Nor did it attempt to stimulate them by introducing such phrases as "top of the morning" or "bottoms up."

There is nothing wrong, of course, in attempting to motivate a child, and any insightful teacher would indeed recognize and make provisions for an unmotivated pupil. The reasons for the lack of motivation must be discovered, and a sequence for stimulating motivation, itself, can be developed. Behavior modification techniques are often helpful. The point is, however, that too much devotion to the child and his presumed lack of motivation often siphons the teacher's attention away from the instructional task. The net result is an ineffective sequence. At first glance, this written sequence may indeed *appear* valid, but if one subtracts all of the beginning motivation steps, the remainder generally is scant. It becomes apparent that in such a sequence there is no genuine attempt to *teach*. To put it differently, the teacher may succeed with motivating (even when it is not needed!), but fail with instruction.

All this does not negate that the actual *materials* used in preparing the instructional sequence for the child ought to be motivating. The teacher *should* use magic markers to write large and colorful math examples and to draw pictures needed for illustrating and clarifying. Also, it is motivating to *personalize* the lesson, the topic, the examples, the theme, etc. The key here is that any vehicle designed to motivate the pupil must be 100 percent task-related and should never supplant or postpone instruction itself.

In writing instructional sequences, therefore, the teacher does well to assume that motivation is present. Certainly there must be at least one child who is already motivated to learn but desperately needs systematic instruction. In the current vogue of "letting the child do his own thing," we must never forget that the handicapped learner has already demonstrated that he cannot learn on his own; therefore, for him, instructional intervention based upon task analysis is of paramount importance.

Identify Sequential Components

Sequential components make up the mortar for building instructional sequences. Immediately upon stipulating the instructional objective (and noting the prerequisite entering behavior), you may be seized with the urge to plunge right into the instructional procedures (that is, to begin formulating the sequential steps). Don't! Before doing this, consider the objective and begin listing pertinent sequential components as fast as you can think of them. At this point the order is not important. In fact, many of the components you initially list may be discarded before you begin to create the actual steps of your sequence. But if you don't list them at the outset, you will not have them as possible choices later. The plan should be to (1) examine the behavioral objective, (2) list all the sequential components you can think of, (3) decide which ones are important to you, and (4) begin to combine them in your sequence. (Combining instructional sequences will be discussed further in Chapters 4 and 10.)

Each component centers around a specific variable: complexity, degree of supervision, degree to which cues are used, length of time, size of the material, etc. The key words for listing components are "from" and "to." There are *general* components which obtain for many sequences (e.g., from concrete to abstract, from small initial doses to larger doses, from proximal stimuli to distal stimuli, from a great deal of supervision to no supervision, from use of cues to fading out the cues).

Besides these, a given behavioral objective will have its own sequential components. They should be identified and incorporated into the written sequence. For example, in teaching a pupil to identify verbs which appear in a series of written sentences, the direction should be from instruction in recognition of action verbs to recognition of state-of-being verbs, from initially depicting actions which the pupil can actually observe to those which he must imagine, from using the terminology "action word" to finally using the term "verb," etc. In teaching the pupil to differentiate auditorially between the long-*a* and short-*a* sounds appearing in one-syllable words, the order should be from words in which the vowel sound is the initial sound (*ache, ax*, etc.) to medial (*bake, tack*, etc.) or possibly final placement. It should proceed from practice in discriminating the pure vowel sounds to isolating them in words, from use of a reference chart tying in a key picture for each sound (e.g., a picture of an apron for the long *a* and a picture of an apple for a short *a*), to producing the sound from memory. This sequence should also move from holding the word for a long time (trying to match the vowel sound being held with the chart's key sound) to pronouncing the word in a natural, nonexaggerated fashion.

The sample sequences demonstrate the following components:

Sample Sequence I ("More Than" or "Less Than")

> from materials to numbers
> from big differences to small differences
> from use of the "superlative" cue to fading out the cue
> from use of the "puppy" or the "big part to the big group" cue to fading out this cue
> from using the cardboard cutout ◀ to writing the sign
> from objects on paper to numbers on paper
> from supervision to independence
> from the teacher reading the "sentence" to the child reading the "sentence."

Sample Sequence II ("Top" and "Bottom")

> from vertical to horizontal
> from a person to a picture of a person
> from a picture to a blank sheet of paper
> from a large picture to a smaller picture
> from cues (the picture) to no cues

Sample Sequence III (s and sm)

> from color cues to no color cues
> from "face" cues to no cues
> from use of chart to no chart
> from the teacher producing the sound to the child producing it
> from exaggerating the sound to speaking normally
> from identifying the pure sound to identifying the sound within one specific nonsense syllable
> from identifying the sound combined with one specific nonsense syllable to identifying it within words.
> from producing the pure sound to producing the sound combined with one specific nonsense syllable
> from producing the sound combined with one specific nonsense syllable to producing the sound within words

The handicapped learner needs support and structure. A consideration of sequentialized components of instructional tasks is a key means of affording him the "cushion" (physically as well as psychologically) he requires.

Become Proficient in Technical Aspects of the Instructional Task

Besides being able to write educational sequences generally, the teacher must also be acquainted with all phases of the given task's requirements. In this way, she will be able to give the child the "fine points." For example, in learning to ride a bicycle, it is easier to balance if one looks straight ahead rather than down, and if one goes a little faster rather than too slowly. Sawing a piece of wood is easier if the pupil stands and works the saw at right angles to the wood. In blending a consonant with a "family" (for example *ay*), the child is helped considerably if we use the letter *s* (which can be held a long time) instead of a plosive letter like *p* (which ends as soon as it is pronounced). When teaching the order relationship of two adjacent letters, it is easier initially to drill on "what letter comes after___," than "what letter comes before___" since it is unlikely that the child can recite the alphabet backwards as competently as he can forward. Despite the fact that most phonics instructional programs begin with the short vowels (generating easy three-letter words), it may, in fact, be of considerable technical assistance to the pupil if he is taught the long vowels first. There are two reasons for this: (1) Any given long vowel sounds totally different from another (this is not the case with short vowels), and (2) the sounds of the long vowels are recapitulated in their alphabet names.

When learning how to subtract two-place numbers with exchange,* the child will generally find an example like

$$\begin{array}{r} 41 \\ -19 \\ \hline \end{array}$$

easier than

$$\begin{array}{r} 45 \\ -17 \\ \hline \end{array}$$

(That is,

$$\begin{array}{r} 11 \\ -9 \\ \hline \end{array}$$

can be solved with relative ease by either counting "down" from eleven or "up" from nine, whereas the big difference between the two amounts in

$$\begin{array}{r} 15 \\ -7 \\ \hline \end{array}$$

may very well make it harder.)

In the "more than" or "less than" sequence (Sample Sequence I), the cardboard cutout was introduced in deference to the possibility that the pupil might find the actual writing of the unfamiliar sign somewhat difficult. In the "top" and "bottom" sequence (Sample Sequence II), the tiltboard was deemed to be a supportive gradual mediator between the vertical and horizontal planes. In the *s* and *sm* sequence (Sample Sequence III), it was no accident that the blend *sm* was chosen as the first *s*-blend, rather than others such as *st* or *sp* which do not blend as smoothly with the rest of the word.

Do Not Merely Present, Teach!

If it is true (in keeping with a major tenet of this book) that the heart of teaching is imparting knowledge or a skill, then this final guideline

---

*Throughout this book, the term "exchange" (an older term) will be used interchangeably with the more current term "regrouping." They are virtually synonymous, except that regrouping sometimes has the additional connotation of "expanded notation," e.g.,

42 = 4 tens + 2 ones = 3 tens + 12 ones
29 = 2 tens + 9 ones = 2 tens +   9 ones

must be considered the heart of instructional sequencing. Most adequate learners can learn when material is merely presented to them. The excellent student may even be able to discover for himself that, in the numeral *25*, the *2* represents *2* tens and the *5* is really *5* ones. Out-of-school experiences with equivalencies in money and making change (quarters, dimes, and nickels) might well have given him this understanding; and he may even have made the generalization into other two-place numerals.

For most of the other children, a simple demonstration or verbalization by the teacher will serve to coalesce their previous experiences; and they, too, will understand what the digits *6* and *7* in the numeral *67* represent.

The handicapped learner (in any particular area) is the one who doesn't "get it" when the teacher has only said it or shown it. He needs more than that. The instructional sequence is the "more" that he needs.

How does the teacher who has written a sequence decide whether or not she is really teaching and not just presenting? There are two major pitfalls. First, if the sequence does not require the child to *do* anything, the teacher can have no certainty that the child has learned anything or that she has taught anything. If, in a sequence to "teach the difference between *s* and *sm*," the steps enumerate only what the teacher will do and say (e.g., (1) the teacher puts *s* and *sm* on the board, (2) she voices the sound of each, (3) she gives a word or several words beginning with *s* or *sm* as examples for each), then she is merely presenting the material, not teaching it. On the basis of this "teaching," the sequence writer may now expect the child to demonstrate what he has "learned" by doing the typical workbook exercise. This usually requires him to look at a picture, perhaps of a smoking chimney, and choose correctly from two or more answers. He must now mark an X in the box labeled "*sm*" rather than "*s*" or "*sp*," etc. This, then, becomes the second pitfall to avoid. It is an example of expecting the child to do something *without* instruction. If he can do it, then he didn't need any teaching in this area; he may already have known how to differentiate *s* from *sm*, or, perhaps he was able to make the correct generalization merely from presentation. On the other hand, the child who responds to the worksheet by saying, "I don't understand," or who tries to complete the task and gets almost all of the items wrong, or perhaps just goes through the page and merely marks an X on anything he sees, is the candidate for a good instructional sequence.

There are additional pitfalls which are extensions of this latter one. That is, there are other practices in which teachers may unwittingly engage that are tantamount to expecting the child to demonstrate that which he has not yet been taught. One such pitfall is starting at too advanced a point. The initial step in the sequence must be based entirely upon the pupil's entering behavior with particular emphasis upon the *degree* of mastery. For example, if the pupil has a firm grasp of the fives multiplication table (that is, he can answer any randomly selected example—7 x 5 = ?; 9 x 5 = ?; 3 x 5 = ?—quickly and accurately), whether the five appears as the multiplier or multiplicand, can perform from visual and oral stimuli, understands the multiplication facts with respect to materials such as nickels and pennies as well as with numbers, then one may proceed immediately to use this skill in teaching the sixes table (e.g., "seven sixes" is the same as "seven fives" plus "seven ones"). If, however, he has only "a little piece" of the fives table (e.g., makes occasional errors; has to take time to "figure it out"; when pressed, does not "stick to his guns"); then, if it were still deemed to the pupil's benefit to launch the six times table, the sequence would have to go along at a slower pace, with considerable supportive measures (e.g., use of concrete materials, utilization of cues, provision for more teacher supervision, simultaneous strengthening of the fives table, or perhaps using an alternative strategy which is not based upon knowledge of the fives). Similarly, the pupil who finds it difficult to follow oral commands will more likely be successful with three- or four-word sentences initially than with those involving ten or more words.

A further extension of this practice would be those instances in which the sequential steps (especially the beginning ones) go beyond the scope of the behavioral objective. If a sequence is being designed to teach a pupil how to measure to the inch and the half inch with a ruler, clearly it would be illogical to start with the quarter inch or eighth inch.

Another pitfall to be avoided is the "recipe approach." It is possible to write instructional sequences which are technically correct, yet are non-supportive as far as the handicapped learner is concerned. Consider the cook's printed recipe. Obviously the steps are ordered, and the experienced cook will have no difficulty in following them. But the novice may not understand the meaning of "baste," "simmer," and "diced," and may require specific instruction in how to knead dough and to "fold in" beaten egg whites.

A carpentry shop may have the steps for sawing a piece of wood listed on a work chart in perfect sequence. However, if these do not take into account the child with perceptual and/or coordination difficulties, the pupil who needs help in actually gripping the saw, sawing on a straight line, making the initial groove, and in sawing for long periods of time, will not find this kind of sequence adequate.

Have you ever ordered something which requires assembly? You open the carton. There, in a corner of it, is the instruction sheet for assembly of the contents. They are in perfect order. And yet, you, along with many other "normal" learners, may encounter considerable difficulty in following these sequential instructions. They simply are not sufficiently supportive.

In academic areas, instructional sequences must show a sensitivity for handicapped learners. Just as it is necessary to *teach* the inexperienced cook the actual motions involved in kneading, and to include some supportive steps in a carpentry task analysis, instructional sequences in arithmetic and in phonics must likewise reflect teaching the needs of a handicapped learner.

For example, the "more than" and "less than" sequence (Sample Sequence I) utilized writing the correct sign, < or > , between two groups of *objects* which were placed on paper before writing it between *numbers on that very paper*. It was felt that using the same sheet of paper "held it all together" for the pupil. The *s* and *sm* sequence (Sample Sequence III) offered the "*sm*iling face" and "sad face" cues, a definitely supportive measure.

Finally, one must avoid substituting a variety of activities in lieu of an instructional sequence. At times, a teacher submits an instructional "sequence" which has the aura of appropriateness, since every "step" is related to the aim. Stated simply, there are no unrelated points—and this, of course, is to be admired. A closer inspection, however, may reveal that these are really not "steps," since one point does not lead into another. The order is entirely arbitrary, and there has been no attempt to *teach* any of the points. For example, there are many ways of teaching (or to be more precise, *practicing*) subtraction with exchange. One could construct a place-value chart in conjunction with squared material; one could use coins; one could use an abacus; one could practice the written algorism; one could read and solve problems requiring subtraction with renaming. None of these activities, in themselves, actually *teach* the handicapped learner, which is the stipulated aim. For example, no strategy for recognition of when or how renaming is necessary was offered.

Consider the following sequential steps:

1. The child seated at his desk, on which is placed a blank piece of 8½" by 11" paper, is told to color the top part blue and the bottom green.

2. Another piece of paper is placed on the child's desk and he is told to look at the top and then at the bottom.

3. Another piece of paper is placed on the child's desk. A rubber mouse is placed in the center of the paper. He is told to make the mouse go to the top of the paper for cheese.

4. Another piece of paper is placed on the child's desk and he is told to place a plastic green arrow on top and a red arrow at the bottom.

Although those "steps" are all related to the behavioral objective mentioned in Sample Sequence II, they in no way *teach* this objective. Their very order is irrelevant, and, in fact, they are simply four individual "practicing" activities.

A variety of activities should indeed be utilized, but only as substeps at a given point (generally, at the last step). In other words, a particular step in an instructional sequence may well require massive practice in a variety of ways, but variety, per se, can never be a substitute for instruction.

All of these guidelines can be encapsulated in two prepotent principles: (1) Stipulate that the given child is absolutely ready for your sequence, but that (2) he is utterly incapable of learning it without specific instruction. The first insures that the teacher will not spend time in needlessly reviewing prerequisites; in projecting extraneous material which, however creative and clever in appearance, is totally irrelevant; or in attempting to motivate the already motivated child. The second enhances the likelihood that the teacher will not substitute a variety of unconnected and unordered activities (albeit pertinent to the lesson's aim) for ordered step-by-step instruction; will not offer a technically correct yet unmodified, nonindividualized, and nonsupportive recipe; will identify sequential components of the instructional module; will become aware of the technical aspects of the task; and above all, will show a healthy respect for the difference between teaching and merely presenting.

CHAPTER FOUR

How to Combine Sequential Components

All the guidelines for creating instructional sequences have just been presented. We are now ready to focus upon the actual construction of sequences.

As mentioned previously, sequential components are the mortar with which the instructional sequence is constructed. A given behavioral objective generates a list of sequential components. This array must be examined, and those components deemed pertinent, selected. Then the teacher must combine these components in some logical fashion, thereby creating the instructional steps.

Consider the following components for teaching a pupil to erase neatly:

Behavioral Objective

When given several words written with a No. 2 pencil on a sheet of 8½" by 11" paper, the pupil will be able to erase them neatly using a regular pencil's eraser.

Components

1. from small amounts to large amounts
2. from erasing lighter writing to erasing darker writing
3. from using art gum (sometimes called "soap eraser") to using the pencil's eraser
4. from using an eraser on a thicker pencil to one on a regular-size pencil
5. from erasing on oak tag (the material of which file folders are made) to erasing on paper (paper is thinner)
6. from the teacher's verbal cues to no cues

7. from drill in selecting a clean rather than a smudgy eraser to no drill
8. from the teacher physically guiding pupil's hand to no guidance
9. from erasing words written in an open space to words written within a confined area
10. from erasing sand-writing (or chalk writing) to erasing on paper

Suppose, after formulating these ten components, you decide to omit components 4, 7, 8, 9, and 10. (Remember, this is a question of opinion. Other teachers' judgment may dictate a different choice and yet create equally effective sequences.)

The sequence could then be written in this fashion:

1. Write a small word with a light stroke (with a No. 2 pencil) on a piece of oak tag. Give the pupil an art gum eraser and instruct him to erase the word. Provide verbal cues (e.g., "Hold the oak tag"; "Rub back and forth lightly").

2. Write darker (still using a No. 2 pencil). Continue to use oak tag, a small word, an art gum eraser, and verbal cues.

3. Write several longer words with a dark stroke. Continue to use oak tag, art gum, and verbal cues.

4. Switch to a pencil's eraser and begin fading out verbal cues. Still use oak tag.

5. Switch from oak tag to paper and omit all verbal cues.

It should be pointed out that the sequential steps presented in this book seem to move very fast. In actuality, a given sequence—such as the one just presented—may well take many lessons to complete in view of needed repetitions, modifications, and in deference to the gradualness with which each component may have to be faded out. The concept of sequencing, though, is held together better by formulating it in this brisk tempo rather than by endeavoring to enumerate and to describe the entire series of anticipated lessons. Notice also that at each step, the pupil is required to do something. If this were not the case, we would be presenting instead of teaching.

Note that this sequence combined *all* of the chosen components in the first step. Each ensuing step finalized—or began fading out—one or more components, so that at the last step, all that remained was the pupil performing the stated behavioral objective. The choice as to the order of finalizing (or fading out) rests entirely with the individual teacher. The foregoing illustrative sequence selected component number 2 (lighter to darker) as the first one to be finalized. Other teachers may elect a different component (e.g., number 5 [oak tag to paper] or number 3 [art gum eraser to pencil eraser]) as the first one to bring to completion. It all depends upon what the sequence writer deems most supportive.

Another way to combine sequential components is to use many—but not all—of them in the first step, begin fading them out, and, at some later step(s), inject the remaining component(s). For example, if we had desired to include component number 4 (from using an eraser on a thicker pencil to one on a regular-size pencil), the sequence could have been written in this way:

1. Write a small word with a light stroke (with a No. 2 pencil) on a piece of oak tag. Give the pupil an art gum eraser and instruct him to erase the word. Provide verbal cues (e.g., "Hold the oak tag"; "Rub back and forth lightly").

2. Write darker (still using a No. 2 pencil). Continue to use oak tag, a small word, an art gum eraser, and verbal cues.

3. Write several longer words with a dark stroke. Continue to use oak tag, art gum, and verbal cues.

4. Switch from the art gum to a thick pencil eraser and begin to fade out verbal cues. Still use oak tag.

5. Switch from oak tag to paper. Use fewer verbal cues.

6. Switch from thick pencil to regular-size pencil and omit all verbal cues.

In this particular case, given the fact that one wished to include both components number 3 (art gum to pencil's eraser) and number 4 (eraser on a thick pencil to one on a regular pencil), it would have been patently impossible to include *all* the selected components in the first step. That is, if the pupil is using art gum, he cannot possibly use a pencil eraser at the same time.

There is still another appropriate way to combine sequential components. It involves a sequence within a sequence. Consider the same instructional goal of erasing. The teacher may view a particular variable as paramount. Her strategy would then isolate this variable, break it into two (or possiby three) stages, and utilize identical strategies at each stage. Suppose the paramount variable selected was that of hardness of writing material's surface. The teacher would then reason, "I would like to teach him the entire act of erasing on oak tag first, then on thinner material (say, an index card), and finally on regular writing paper."

The sequence would enfold in this manner:

1. Using oak tag on which one small word has been written with a light stroke (No. 2 pencil), give the pupil art gum and instruct him to erase, providing verbal cues.

2. Write darker (No. 2 pencil). Continue using oak tag, a small word, art gum, and verbal cues.

3. Instead of a small word, write several longer ones. Continue using oak tag, dark writing, art gum, and verbal cues.

4. Substitute a regular pencil eraser for the art gum. Continue with oak tag, dark writing, several large words, and verbal cues.

5. Now omit cues. Still use oak tag, pencil eraser, dark writing, and several large words.

6. Repeat Steps 1 through 5 using an index card instead of the oak tag.

7. Repeat Steps 1 through 5 using regular writing paper instead of the index card.

In summary, the teacher, when given a behavioral objective, should begin to list sequential components simply in the order in which they occur to her. Then she should choose the ones to be included in the sequence, and finally, begin to combine them. There are three acceptable strategies for combining sequential components:

1. Put them *all* together in the first step; then begin bringing each to completion, one by one.

2. Put *most* of them in the first step; then begin bringing them to completion, but insert the other(s) at some intermediate step. Continue finalizing one by one.

3. Decide upon *one* overall variable embodied in a given component. Break this variable into several parts (usually two or three). Treat each part as a sequence in itself. The sequential steps under the first part will then be repeated under the remaining part(s), thereby producing a sequence within a sequence.

CHAPTER FIVE

Behavioral Objectives, Entering Behavior, and Assessment

The generally accepted model for task analysis includes four elements: behavioral objective, entering behavior, instructional procedure, and assessment. Instructional procedure consists of the sequential steps themselves. This book is devoted entirely to that aspect: It offers instruction in writing the sequential steps, given the behavioral objective and entering behavior. Nevertheless, becoming a skilled sequence designer can be achieved only by understanding all four aspects and their interrelationships.

Behavioral Objective

The term "behavioral objective" (often called "instructional objective") coincides with the traditional concepts of the lesson's aim. There are, however, some important differences. In the past, it was quite acceptable to list as a geography lesson's aim, "to develop an understanding of the grid lines of a map." Today, one would take issue with this choice of words, since it does not specify what the pupil is expected to *do* as a result of instruction. A more acceptable word choice would be: "When given ten points of longitude and latitude intersection—each coordinate ending in a 5 or a zero (e.g., 50° North and 75° East)—the pupil will be able to locate them on a Mercator map." Aims, goals, and general objectives are often vaguely stated, quite broad in scope, and frequently do not extract any observable behavior. For example, what is the pupil supposed to do following a course of instruction whose aim was "to develop a deep appreciation of Tchaikowsky's music"?

A behavioral objective can be stated precisely, stipulating clearly observable behavior, and still be ill-conceived with respect to the child's needs. Consider an instructional objective whose terminal behavior consists of looking up words in the dictionary. There is nothing vague about that. It tells exactly what the learner is supposed to do following instruction: He must look up given words in a dictionary. (Of course, one should specify how many words and their reading level, what kind of dictionary, whether the stimulus consists of oral or written words, etc. Nevertheless the very phrase "to look up words in the dictionary" denotes considerable specificity regarding what the child is expected to do following instruction.) Suppose that the pupil has had neither experience nor instruction in alphabetizing, and that he does not know the alphabet in perfect order. That is, he may be able to recite it or write it starting with the letter *a*, but he cannot readily answer questions such as, "What letter comes after *s*?" "What letter comes before *d*?" "Is *y* in the beginning, middle, or end of the alphabet?" etc.

In such instances, the teacher's thorough knowledge of the task (which, naturally, is an essential ingredient in task analysis) would dictate that she "sequence down" (i.e., break the original skill down into sequentialized prerequisite subskills). Of course, a very gifted learner may well be able to learn letter recognition, letter order, alphabetizing, and dictionary work all at one time. Not so with the handicapped learner, and *he* is the pupil the teacher must constantly keep in mind as she develops a feeling for creating precise yet supportive instructional sequences. In sequencing down, the teacher realizes that alphabetizing comes before locating words in a dictionary, and, that knowing what letter comes before or after a given letter and/or does a given letter fall in the beginning, middle, or end of the alphabet precedes alphabetizing. Based upon this knowledge, the teacher would then prepare a sequence for "before" and "after" (and/or "beginning, middle, or end" of the dictionary). When this terminal objective has been reached, she would prepare a sequence for teaching alphabetizing skills. Upon successful completion of this (by some observable terminal behavior on the part of the pupil), she could finally launch a sequence dealing with locating words in a dictionary.

This ability to break a task down into its prerequisite tasks will serve the teacher in good stead throughout the curriculum. For example, suppose that one desires to teach a pupil how to add mixed numbers with unlike denominators (e.g., 6-7/8 + 3-3/4 + 4-1/2). The pupil should already know how to reduce to lowest terms (6/8 = ?) and how to add mixed numbers with like denominators (e.g., 5-3/4 + 6-1/4 + 7-3/4). The ability to add mixed numbers with like denominators, however, requires (for sums of one or greater) that the pupil be able to change improper fractions to mixed numbers (e.g., 9/4 = 2-1/4, and 5-3/2 = 6-1/2). This, in turn, presupposes the ability to distinguish between mixed numbers, (6-1/2), proper fractions, (1/4), and improper fractions (9/4).

Theoretically, a teacher could devise a marathon sequence beginning with letter recognition and ending with dictionary skills. The flaws here are that (1) it would take too long to prepare; (2) it would take too long to complete; (3) if "branching" or some modification had to be programed into it in deference to signals which the learner is sending, then a great deal of the sequence would have to be rewritten (this, by the way, is an example of diagnostic teaching); (4) because the terminal goal is so far away, both teacher and pupil may become discouraged, since neither experiences a sense of completion; and (5) because of its length, tangential considerations are more likely to crop up and enthusiasm wane. Moreover, the massive appearance, itself, can seem overwhelming to the teacher and any colleague with whom she wishes to share the sequence. This last point can provide a hint as to whether or not a given sequence might require sequencing down. Does it have too many steps? As a rule of thumb, most instructional sequences can be prepared utilizing between eight and twelve steps. If a given sequence has twenty, thirty, or more steps, it is a good bet that it can be broken down into several prerequisite sequences, each of more manageable duration.

At the other end of the spectrum, a behavioral objective may seem too limited in scope. Consider Sample Sequence III, which involves differentiating between *s* and *sm*. In a sense, the subject matter involved appears almost trivial. It should be pointed out, however, that if the teacher's aim is simple and definite enough, it is more likely that her thinking will be focused upon relevant, supportive, sequential steps. Later, more abstract subject areas can be approached.

It must be obvious that recognizing and producing the *s* and *sm* sounds is a "splinter skill." As an isolated sequence, it would have little meaning for the child who does not generalize easily. It isn't likely that even a superb young learner could make *all* the generalizations necessary to render this specific skill a useful one. However, building upon this sequence to include *every* *s* blend and to teach the child sequentially to differentiate among them, builds toward the ultimate goal of decoding new words phonetically. Similarly, when the teacher prepares an instructional sequence whose aim is that the child produce the cursive letter *l*, she knows, of course, that finally the child will be taught to write words, sentences, and paragraphs ideationally in cursive script. In organizing her thinking to prepare the sequence for the cursive letter *l*, she develops her own skills in following through with further sequences geared towards the final goal. The teacher recognizes that the individual letters thus taught will be linked to form words, then sentences, and finally paragraphs. First, the material is copied (from a paper on the desk, then from the chalkboard, and ultimately from oral dictation). When competency has been achieved, the child's creative writing will be done in cursive script.

If it seems to you that the above is really only simple common sense and not different from the way any good penmanship workbook is arranged, you are quite correct. But recall our maxim, "avoid the recipe approach"; and remember that the handicapped learner will probably require insightful modifications: extra practice, initial short doses of written work, more experience in tracing, actual physical guidance by the teacher grasping his writing hand, directional and/or color-cuing, specially printed paper, cuing for correct word space (finger distance), etc.

Since much of the literature regarding task analysis comes to us from psychologists, the written instructional sequence often exudes a scientific aura which can overwhelm, confuse, and finally discourage teachers. Some teachers are led to believe that a sequence can't possibly be of any value if it is written simply. The scientific semblance, if it exists at all, is to be found in the written behavioral objectives. This is so because one is attempting to define *precisely* what the child will finally do as a result of instruction. It may even be interpreted as a subtle attempt to chide teachers for having been somewhat imprecise in the past. This portion of the sequence generally contains a stipulated frequency of correct response (e.g., when shown a list of twenty three-letter short-*e* words and twenty three-letter short-*a* words in random order, the child will read 90 percent of them correctly within 90 seconds.)

Now, it is true that for some objectives such as decoding, reading comprehension, arithmetic computation, etc., it may be a good idea to stipulate correct-incorrect ratios. And, in general, behavioral objectives should be stated in a very specific way: "When *given (shown, commanded to, presented with, asked to differentiate, etc.)* . . . the pupil will *write (solve, identify, assemble, construct, match).* . . ." In other words, *under specific conditions, the learner will exhibit a particular terminal behavior* (thereby demonstrating to you—and to any other competent witness—that the instructional objective has been reached.)

In other instances, however, these are patently unnecessary. For example, a child can either ride a bicycle or he can't; he can write a well-formed and properly sized capital cursive letter *H* or he can't; he can tell time correct to the hour and half hour or he can't. In fact, in these cases, the behavioral objective does not really differ from the aim (traditionally couched in relatively general terms). It does not even have to be written out and, more likely than not, can be found in the final step(s) of the sequence.

There is another aspect of task analysis which may contribute to excessive use of jargonese. It is the recognition that any instructional task is derived from developmental processes (e.g., perception, motor responses, body image, etc.) and that these should definitely be considered when evaluating the child's entering behavior and in the adaptation of possible modifications of the instructional procedure. Fine. There is some danger, however, beginning teachers may erroneously assume that, therefore, all behavioral objectives must be expressed in terms of these developmental processes.

The resulting confusion can be illustrated by an anecdote. One teacher, when asked to devise a sequence for teaching a child to ride a bicycle, wrote the following: "*Behavioral Objective*: to determine the degree of visual-motor development and physical integration to enable the child to mount and pedal a bike while maintaining balance and directionality." To which the instructor inscribed the incisive comment: "Wow!"

Entering Behavior

The entering behavior aspect of task analysis focuses upon the student as he presents himself for instruction. The concept of "readiness" is apropos here. Is he ready for the task neurologically? Perceptually? Maturationally? Physically? Motivationally? With respect to language development? Cognitively? In terms of independent functioning? Does he have the prerequisite attention span? Are the responses called for by the instructional procedure within his repertoire? Even when all of these states of readiness exist (or, if not, when they can be dealt with via modifications within the sequence), the key question must still be asked: Has he attained the necessary academic level and past learnings inherent in the behavioral objective?

This, of course, is the difference between "teaching arithmetic" and "teaching the child." The best designed sequence, one in which all steps are relevant to the instructional objective, spaced appropriately, ordered logically, written with optimal clarity, and supportive in nature, will yet prove worthless if the learner has not mastered the prerequisite skills. In such instances, the handicapped learner, whose ego is already fragile, is actually being programed for additional failure experiences! It would be much more fruitful for the teacher, aware of the prerequisites of the task and equally cognizant of the child's entering behavior (and the successful teacher must indeed heed both of these), to launch an alternate sequence having as its behavioral objective the very prerequisite skills of the original sequence.

The pupil may have already mastered not only the prerequisite skills, but the terminal objective as well. Stated simply, the projected lessons may be too easy for him, since he can perform the behavioral objective prior to any instruction. There is nothing wrong in arranging success-assured experiences or in preparing review activities. In fact, many pupils benefit by these at times. The point, though, is that the teacher should know "where the child is at," and must not, as a result of her own imprecision, engage in what is tantamount to pawning off "review" or "training for independence," or "failure-free activities," as teaching new knowledge or a skill.

There is a painless way for the teacher to "test" a pupil—or a class—immediately prior to initiation of the sequence to see whether or not the terminal objective has already been mastered. It involves the teacher demonstrating her own "failure" in a given area. Say to the pupils: "There are many things that I can't do. Can you think of any?" (Elicit from the pupils a task such as touching the ceiling. Jump as high as you can and really try to touch the ceiling.) "See. I can't do that.

"Now there is something hard I can think of that I believe *you* can't do. Here are some nickels and dimes." (Put coins within reach of pupils.) "Can you give me change for a quarter?"

On the one hand, if the pupils know how to do this, then they do not need to go through that sequence. On the other hand, if they cannot do it, it proves to the teacher and to them that they do indeed need systematic instruction in that skill. This technique is especially effective when the teacher is certain that the appropriate entering behavior has already been attained (e.g., recognition of the coins, knowledge of the value of each, the concept of making change, the ability to add fives and tens) and if the sequence itself is relatively brief. The teacher will then be in position to utilize the pupils' failure (which they have just exhibited in a relatively nonthreatening environment) in leading them to rise to the challenge: "OK. So you can't make change of a quarter now. But I know that you are absolutely ready to learn how to do it. At the end of this lesson, I'll bet you'll all be able to do it."

Thus there is an inescapable relationship between the behavioral objective and the pupil's entering behavior. In fact, teacher-training programs should include developing an appreciation for—and skill in—articulating the immediately prior learning called for by a given behavioral objective. For example, a handicapped learner who is nevertheless deemed ready to learn how to alphabetize twenty one-syllable words, each beginning with a different letter, should already recognize and be able to name all the letters of the alphabet and should have some "handle" on their order. (That is, he should be able to recite the alphabet, possibly by virtue of having been exposed to the "ABC" song). If he does not present this entering behavior, then he is miles away from the behavioral objective. Similarly, learning to subtract a two-place number with exchange (e.g., 42 − 29), demands prior knowledge of subtraction without exchange, of place value (this would have been encountered in addition of two-place numbers, which is easier than—and therefore would have been taught prior to—subtraction), and of the concept of subtraction. If all of this has not been learned previously, then the instant behavioral objective is poorly chosen. If the child whom we are endeavoring to instruct to write the cursive capital letter *G* does not know how to grasp a pencil, cannot write easier letters such as *l* or *i*, and cannot even draw a reasonably straight line or a circle, then why on earth would one plan to *begin* instruction with the *G*?

If the pupil is about to be taught how to conjugate the French verb, *parler*, there are many prerequisite items of knowledge (e.g., visual and auditory discrimination of *parlons* and *parlez*, the meaning of verbs, the ability to identify verbs, the concept of translation). However, *immediately* prior to this should have been the ability to stipulate and recognize the order, number, and gender of verb forms (even from his study of English grammar) in conjunction with their respective pronouns:

	Singular	Plural
1st Person	I talk	we talk
2nd Person	you talk	you talk
3rd Person	he ⎫ she ⎭ talks	they talk

There is one aspect of task analysis which unwittingly lends itself to imprecision regarding the *immediate* entering behavior suggested by a behavioral objective. It is that model which suggests that the sequence designer go back "to the very beginning." For example, a task analysis for telling time correct to the minute would require awareness of these prerequisite skills:

1. Recognizing the numerals *1* to *12* auditorially and visually.
2. Naming the numerals *1* to *12*.
3. Recognizing and naming the numerals *1* to *12* in a circle (on a clock's face) as well as on a straight line.
4. Counting from *1* to *60*.
5. Distinguishing the long hand from the short hand, etc.

There is undoubtedly some value in tracing a given task to its origin. The teacher who does this develops a healthy respect for all of the past learning required by the terminal objective. But in endeavoring to consider *all* of them, one may inadvertently lose sight of the *immediately preceding* ones. Our handicapped learner certainly will have to master the five skills listed above, but to include them in this sequence will virtually insure that our sequence will have at least fifty steps and will take inordinate amounts of time to complete. Again, the handicapped learner who has *not* mastered these five skills is so far away from the behavioral objective of telling time to the minute, that it renders ludicrous the initiation of this sequence. Indeed, what would a handicapped learner need to know immediately prior to learning to tell time to the minute? Telling time to the hour and to the half hour should be absolutely mastered first, and this could lead *directly* into telling time to the minute.

What about the *usefulness* of a given instructional objective? Having seen the necessity for matching the behavioral objective with the entering behavior, we are now ready to look at "the other side of the coin." Simply stated, it is this: Even when the entering behavior enables the pupil to master a particular behavioral objective, if his current status prevents him from benefiting by the acquisition of it, then its selection would be inappropriate. For example, alphabetizing and dictionary skills are often used in conjunction with spelling activities. The class is given a list of 10 to 20 words to learn over the week; and part of the reinforcement of learning (as well as building of vocabulary) is to look up in the dictionary and write the meanings of some of the spelling words. Perhaps the poorest spellers are using only words from their week's reading assignment as their spelling list (frequently from a linguistic reader, e.g.: *sip, ship, clip*). These children may know the alphabet and can be taught by means of a dictionary-skills sequence, to find some of *their* spelling words in the dictionary, just as the more able spellers in the class do. However, if their reading level is so low that they can in no way read the definition, the instructional goal may be a useless, eminently frustrating one and, in fact, constitute another example of a "splinter skill."

Having said this, let us now point out that, in the interest of enhancing a given pupil's self-concept, the teacher may choose even in these instances, to forge ahead. In other words, there are times in which the pupil should be offered instruction in a behavioral objective even though all prerequisites for it have not been thoroughly mastered. Some enabling modifications would be for our poor reader merely to locate the word in the dictionary, and his "buddy," a more able reader, to read its definition to him. Similarly, he can use his "dictionary skills" to locate a city's name on a map's alphabetized list of cities or a person's name in a simplified telephone book. *When* and *how* to utilize this approach are totally dependent upon the teacher's sensitivity to the emotional needs of the pupil, flexibility, skill in (and dedication to the principle of) individualization—and sheer creativity.

Good teachers have utilized this supportive strategy for years. Isn't the experience chart a vehicle by which the nonwriter may nevertheless gain experience in "writing" creatively? Many slow learners have been systematically led toward multiplication despite the fact that they have not yet mastered the prerequisite basic addition facts. There are two persuasive reasons for teaching in this manner: (1) It is motivational. (The pupil is not being held back. He's covering the same ground as his "normal" peers.) (2) The higher objective frequently gives functional practice in the area of deficit (e.g., multiplying 79 x 5 requires the pupil—at the last step—to add 35 + 4.)

Modification is the needed ingredient. Experience charts, duplicated material, and the tape recorder are some ways in which writing can be bypassed (provided, of course, that penmanship itself is not the instructional objective). In other cases, the deficit can actually be strengthened through modification (e.g., specially preboxed paper to facilitate the writing of numbers in column addition). Having the multiplication tables retrievable in an exposed matrix chart facilitates rote memory of these facts even while the pupil uses them to solve the algorism. The following multiplication matrix can also be used for division.

Multiplication Table

X	0	1	2	3	4	5	6	7	8	9
0	0	0	0	0	0	0	0	0	0	0
1	0	1	2	3	4	5	6	7	8	9
2	0	2	4	6	8	10	12	14	16	18
3	0	3	6	9	12	15	18	21	24	27
4	0	4	8	12	16	20	24	28	32	36
5	0	5	10	15	20	25	30	35	40	45
6	0	6	12	18	24	30	36	42	48	54
7	0	7	14	21	28	35	42	49	56	63
8	0	8	16	24	32	40	48	56	64	72
9	0	9	18	27	36	45	54	63	72	81

While bringing the pupil who has still not mastered the basic addition facts forward into addition with exchange, it is supportive to provide crutches (strategies, cues, etc.) In fact, it is sound pedagogy to provide specific instruction for these very crutches. For example, the algorism

$$\begin{array}{r} 29 \\ +13 \\ \hline \end{array}$$

should be approached by showing the pupil how to "count up" from the highest number to the answer. Teach him to *think* "nine," and then *add* "ten," "eleven," "twelve," using the three fingers he holds up or the three little lines he marks near his example.

Mastery (i.e., memory) of these basic addition facts can be further facilitated by systematically emphasizing specific number combinations in the daily arithmetic lessons. If you want to reinforce memory of "doubles," then all the "new" addition examples should be made up of "doubles." Even head the paper with "reminders" of the doubles combinations:

$$2 + 2 = \quad 3 + 3 = \quad 4 + 4 = \quad \ldots 9 + 9 =$$

Then provide practice in the "new" addition with exchange:

$$\begin{array}{ccccc} 24 & 36 & 27 & 29 & 43 \\ +14 & +46 & +37 & +19 & +13 \\ \hline \end{array}$$

The effective teacher must seek to blend the usefulness and the ego-building criteria. Perhaps this is a reflection of the perennial concern with whether the process of teaching is an art or a science. The very title of this book—*Creating Instructional Sequences*—suggests that it is a blend of the two.

Assessment

Assessment goes on throughout the entire sequence. It starts with the entering behavior; one must know the degree of prior attainment the student brings to the educational scene. It permeates the various instructional steps; frequently the pupil will not be able to proceed to the next step unless he has succeeded in the one preceding it. It culminates with an evaluation of the terminal objective; in most instances, this can be assessed by simply observing whether or not the pupil succeeds at the last step of the sequence. To put this differently, the last procedural step is generally an enactment of the stated behavioral objective. There are some pitfalls regarding assessment. The successful teacher will be aware of and will strive to avoid these:

Teachers may give unwitting clues. These include facial expressions, tones of voice, and any other idiosyncratic body language which tends to "give the answer away" in an oral question-answer situation. Other examples of this would be for the teacher to look in the direction of the correct answer (if it is visual in nature), unconsciously mouthing the correct response, providing multiple-choice items in which the correct answer's order is unvaried or in which the alternate choices are patently impossible, and framing a question in such a way that the wording provides a clue (e.g., "If you can guess how many cookies I have in my hand, I'll give you both of them.")

Teachers may fail to take into account the varying degrees of understanding. There are varying degrees of understanding. A pupil may just barely understand, holding on to "just a little piece" of the material being taught; he may understand fairly well but not thoroughly, missing many of the subtleties, ramifications, and conceptualized principles; or grasp completely, achieving a high degree of mastery. The teacher, then, must realize the possibility of the child's knowing and yet not *really* knowing; there are techniques which can take into account these varying degrees of mastery:

Consider an instructional sequence wherein the terminal objective is for the pupil to provide oral answers to questions involving some of the multiplication tables. A pupil who is only partially sure may still produce the right answer. The teacher rewards him immediately. He is satisfied. The teacher, believing that the pupil has learned, is obviously pleased. And most unfortunately, the question-answer period for that item is over. The teacher should train herself *not* to reward—or give any other clue—immediately after the pupil's response, but to wait a few seconds. A pupil who answers the question, "How much is seven times six?" with "forty-two," may follow his initial unsure response with "forty-three," "forty-four," and other such guesses, provided the teacher does not react at once to his first try. It is as though the teacher, by refraining from comment, is asking the child to "stick by his guns." If the pupil really knows the answer, the pause does not throw him off. If the teacher hadn't paused, however, she might never know of his tenuous grasp and would therefore have no reason to initiate remediation.

The kinds of questions a teacher asks can often help to reveal the degree of mastery. A pupil who may handle a "yes-no" question correctly may fail in more thought-provoking ones. A multiple-choice test item generally requires less mastery than does an open-ended question. Generally, essays warrant more thought than do objective-type test items. Asking the pupil to explain how he arrived at an arithmetic example's answer may unearth problems that may not otherwise be evident. It is interesting and helpful to note that in a nurse's tutoring study in which student nurses from disadvantaged areas were tutored in biological sciences by proficient college students, the single most effective instructional method in the opinions of the tutees and the project evaluators was the tutor's request to "explain it back to me."

Certainly, memory is one way of determining degree of grasp. When a child forgets some previously "learned" material quickly, it is highly likely that he never mastered it initially. Although this is the case generally, the teacher should bear in mind that many handicapped learners have problems in this very area—memory. When they forget, it is not necessarily a reflection upon the suitability of the sequence, the quality of the teacher's instruction, or of the degree of the lesson's success. It simply means that these individuals need periodic, systematic review. The principle of overlearning is an essential one for these pupils.

Teachers may read too much into a pupil's answer. At times, a teacher sets up a teaching-learning situation; the pupil is led towards performing a particular instructional objective; but the teacher exaggerates the significance and meaning of the pupil's response, thereby misdiagnosing his true level of achievement. It is not unlike the story told of the researcher who, having trained a flea to hop upon verbal command, proceeds to sever pairs of the flea's legs. At each point he commands, "Hop." The last pair of legs finally severed, the flea does not obey the order, "Hop," whereupon the researcher concludes, "This experiment proves dramatically that when a flea's legs are cut off he becomes deaf!"

Suppose a teacher is instructing a pupil to recognize one object and two objects. The teacher constructs sets of domino cards, say, ten, for each number. She prepares ten cards with one dot $\boxed{\bullet}$ and ten cards with two dots $\boxed{\bullet\bullet}$. After some instruction, the pupil is able to respond with 100 percent accuracy, answering either "one" or "two" when shown a card. Now the teacher may conclude from this that the pupil fully understands "two-ness" and can recognize two objects as distinct from any other number of them. This may, of course, very well be the case. It is also possible, however, that he understands the concept of "one" only, and that his selection of the "two" card was made on the basis of *differentness*: "It is different from *one*, and since the only possibilities dealt with here are *one* and *two*, it must be *two*." To discover the true degree of mastery, the teacher can introduce some three-dot cards $\boxed{\bullet\bullet\bullet}$. The pupil may then show considerable confusion between "two," and "three." The point is that he never fully understood "two," but this became apparent to the teacher only after "three" was introduced.

In photography, there is an axiom which states that a print can never yield more details than does its original negative. Unfortunately, in education, a faulty interpretation of a response's significance can create an erroneous reflection of higher yield than the response which generated it.

Teachers may assess a performance on the basis of invalid criteria. If a test (or the last step of a sequence) requires the pupil to copy twenty sentences from the chalkboard and underline every noun, the pupil who is a slow and erratic copier will likely fail. Question: should he fail English or should he fail copying? Similarly, does a child who cannot talk, necessarily fail reading?

Here one sees the relationship between performance, assessment, entering behavior, and instructional procedures. Clearly, in assessing the entering behavior of a given pupil, impaired modalities must be recognized; these can then be accommodated by means of modifications at the various sequential steps themselves. In this way, not only will optimal feedback be facilitated, but the validity of the sequence will be insured. That is, we will be teaching and measuring that which we purport to be teaching and measuring.

CHAPTER SIX

Subject Matter Variables

The principle of creating instructional sequences applies to all (or at least most) educational experiences, but in different ways and in varying degrees. Perceptual-motor training and psycholinguistic training are the two major areas which, by their very nature, are highly developmental. And so, the authors of various published programs in those fields (e.g., motor training—Newell Kephart, G. N. Getman, Bryant Cratty, Ray Barsch; visual-motor training—Marianne Frostig, Belle Dubnoff; psycholinguistic training—*Peabody Language Development Kits*, Sam and Winifred Kirk, Wilma Jo Bush and Marian Taylor Giles, the *M.W.M. Program*) have adhered extremely well to the concept of sequencing. Therefore, teachers wishing to include these curriculum areas need only to acquire these materials and to master the techniques their authors have described.

Special education, however, does not begin and end with perceptual and language training. On all grade levels, the pupil's curriculum also includes the traditional "Three Rs." There are specific considerations with respect to instructional sequencing which pertain to particular subject areas:

Arithmetic

Although the math processes (addition, subtraction, multiplication, division) have built in procedural steps, these do not supplant supportive sequential components. For example: The procedural steps for adding two-place numbers with exchange are:(1) add all the digits in the ones' column; (2) inspect this partial total; (3) if it consists of a single digit, merely write it under the answer line in the ones' column (if it contains two digits, write the ones' digit in its appropriate column and write the tens' digit in the tens' column above the first addend); and (4) add the digits in the tens' column.

Teachers (and pupils) do indeed have to know these procedural steps. However, to build the total teaching experience around these procedures is inadequate and, in fact, would be a case of presenting rather than teaching. The gifted student might benefit from such an approach, but the handicapped learner needs more support: from use of representative materials to solving algorisms; from a box cue (□) above the tens' column to omitting this prompt; from solving examples with only two addends to solving those with three or more; from having an addition fact matrix available for easy reference to relying solely upon memory of the facts, etc.

The procedural steps themselves may be illustrated on a chart and included as one of the supportive components—"from using the chart as a cue to removal of the chart."

Though most arithmetic texts and workbooks follow some sequential direction, experience has shown that their sequences break down when the more complex concepts of math are initiated, leaving learning gaps too wide for the handicapped learner to bridge on his own. One instance in which this can be seen is in the introduction of division by a two-place divisor. Texts seem to proceed *much* too quickly here, especially ignoring the handicapped learner's initial need to have the divisor "fit" exactly into the dividend (i.e., without requiring a change in the quotient number). In the example—32)918—the "natural" first quotient digit, 3, is too large. The best initial choices of a divisor should consist of digits 1, 2, or 3. In selecting two-place divisors using these digits, the teacher can construct examples by multiplying a preselected two-place quotient and the divisor. This will result in an example which almost always has a dividend of only three places. For effective sequencing, it is better to begin at this level. Some examples that can be considered for use are:

$$32\overline{)992} \qquad\qquad 24\overline{)336}$$

$$34\overline{)408} \qquad\qquad 25\overline{)775}$$

The algorism, 32)992, was derived by first multiplying 32 x 31. The product, 992, becomes the dividend; and the teacher then chooses either of the two factors multiplied to be the divisor.

Another example of too wide a gap frequently occurs in the teaching of addition with exchange. Any math curriculum stipulates quite clearly that adding of two two-place numbers with exchange is taught before adding two three-place numbers with exchange. What is not considered is that the steps involved may be too complicated for the handicapped learner, if he is expected to master simultaneously exchange in the tens' column and in the ones' column—especially when he is just beginning to learn this skill. The teacher must recognize that each case should be mastered separately before combining them. That is, algorisms requiring exchange in the ones' column only

$$
\begin{array}{r}
248 \\
+128 \\
\end{array}
$$

should be introduced first. When that is learned, another type in which the exchange comes *only* in the tens' column can be taught:

$$651$$
$$+153$$

Finally, the procedures for exchange in both the tens' and ones' columns can be mastered.

An antidote for this problem of "gaps" is the teacher's ability to examine all the procedures required in a specific task (e.g., multiplication of 2 two-place numbers) and then to break the example into its various components. At first, have the pupil practice only the first step of a variety of multiplication algorisms, e.g.,

$$32$$
$$\underline{x15}$$
$$0$$

before going on the further steps. (The teacher should always complete the example in the pupil's presence to nurture his perception of the process as a whole.) She might elect to use only examples in which no carrying is required until the order of procedural computations is overlearned:

$$22$$
$$\underline{x13}$$
$$66$$
$$\underline{22}$$
$$286$$

She might then choose to utilize examples wherein only one "carrying" is required.

An appreciation for the hierarchy of complexity of numbers themselves should be developed. Obviously, easier multiplication facts should be taught first, but they should also be *used* first when introducing more advanced multiplication concepts. For example, the twos table and the fives table are easier to remember than are the sixes, sevens, or eights. Therefore, if the pupil is ready to learn to multiply a two-place number by a single digit, then it is better, initially, to utilize the easier tables, e.g.,

$$25 \quad 34 \quad 22$$
$$\underline{x2} \quad \underline{x5} \quad \underline{x5}$$

when teaching this concept, despite the fact that he is already familiar with all the tables.

In most cases, one can readily determine which number combinations are complex and which are relatively simple: Beyond any question, $5 + 5$ is easier than $9 + 6$, $22 + 33$ is easier than $26 + 39$, $1/4 + 1/4$ is easier than $3/8 + 3/6$, and 7×10 is easier than 7×14. However, this is not always so apparent. For example:

$$72$$
$$\underline{-29}$$

is easier than

$$74$$
$$\underline{-16}$$

(since 12 - 9 is easier than 14 - 6). The teacher should also bear in mind that although 0 and 1 "come before" the other numbers, their concept is frequently difficult to grasp. In introducing the place value of two-place numbers, it is more supportive initially to use numbers in the twenties and thirties than in the teens which precede them. This is so because (1) the concept of "one 10" is difficult to grasp, and (2) the transposition of the tens' numerals (19) in relation to the teens "name" (*nine*teen) is confusing.

Penmanship

Penmanship is another subject area which lends itself handily to instructional sequencing. For the very young child with visual-motor problems, a remedial program like Frostig* or Dubnoff** could very well be an introductory phase before formalized penmanship teaching begins. It might be used in conjunction with (or supplementary to) the task of handwriting itself. The teacher of older children, however, must keep in mind the fact that these pupils will frequently regard visual-motor training as "baby stuff." She must then gear her teaching directly toward task-oriented remediation, that is, remediate the visual-motor deficits via teaching penmanship in a highly sequential manner.

A good penmanship workbook is useful, but again, not supportive enough for the handicapped learner. The teacher must assess any given workbook to be sure it is broken down into the small motor-skill steps required, that it begins with the easier letters (e.g., *i*, *e*, *t*), and that it groups similar letters together. Then she must make sure the pupil's motoric movements are correct (or relearned correctly when they are not); here, too, supplementary material is needed. The children manifesting special problems may require more initial guidance, extra practice, and more cues for longer periods of time than would other children. Since copying from the chalkboard is difficult, the teacher will probably have to duplicate her own materials. Many teachers are discovering that easy access to a duplicating machine is basic to instruction of handicapped learners.

It is crucial that the teacher be aware of the technical elements required for good penmanship: (1) letter formation, (2) size, (3) slant, (4) spacing, (5) endings, (6) joining letters, and (7) instructing left-handed pupils, etc.

A simplified capital-letter chart should also be considered. Some capitals are so difficult to master that the handicapped learner may persist in using lower-case letters even when he knows the correct use of capitals. Some of the simplified capital letters are:

B D E F G H I S U V W Z

*The Frostig Program for the Development of Visual Perception, by Marianne Frostig and David Horne (Chicago: Follett, 1964).

**Belle Dubnoff: The Dubnoff Program I—Level I (New York: Teaching Resources, 1969).

These are only suggested modifications of the letters; and, of course, the teacher can make other forms if she deems them simpler. In some cases, when a pupil can form all the letters in his name except the initial capital, there is really no reason why he cannot use a printed (or manuscript) capital instead. When a lower-grade pupil has mislearned manuscript form, the teacher may be well-advised to proceed immediately to cursive writing, rather than have the pupil spend the time and effort required to relearn correct manuscript form. The caution here is to go slowly and make absolutely certain that the pupil is learning (1) the correct cursive form, and (2) the correct motor movements necessary.

Spelling

Spelling—like arithmetic, phonics, penmanship, English usage, etc.—is a skill subject. As such, it has clearly observable behavioral objectives: Any competent witness can easily determine whether or not the learner spells designated words correctly. Hence, it is a subject which is quite suitable for sequencing.

The success of an instructional sequence is intimately linked with the teacher's awareness of what the process of spelling entails and her adeptness in providing cues, strategic reinforcement, and supportive modifications. Above all, the teacher must be aware of the entering behavior of the pupil who is at the readiness stage for learning how to spell. Only then will the scope of her program insure spelling success for the pupil *at his level*. Therefore, besides teaching him multisensory techniques for revisualization ("seeing" the word in the "mind's eye"), the teacher can choose words which, in themselves, facilitate memorization (e.g., words constructed from the same cluster, like: *cat*, *sat*, *scat*, *hat*, etc.). Verbal prompts which help the child recall clusters such as these, and prepare him for listening to a word's initial sound, make a good start towards mastering phonetic spelling. Additional support can be rendered to the younger learner by deliberately choosing his new reading words (since he comes in contact with them on a daily basis) as his weekly spelling words. This is reinforcing to both reading and spelling.

There should also be daily (and varied) classroom activities centered around the spelling words. A pupil who has the necessary skills can be given the task of alphabetizing his words; writing sentences containing them (even writing paragraphs, provided the teacher chooses words centered about a single theme, such as "The Farm," or "City Life," etc.); selecting the correct spelling word to fill the blank space in a sentence; or unscrambling the "mixed up" spelling words (e.g., *atc* becomes *cat*). Sometimes giving each pupil a daily oral test of one or two of his own spelling words and rewarding points or tokens for each correct one will encourage more careful studying.

Each child should be taught—and be proficient in—a good procedural study method. Parents can also be informed about these methods and the need for consistency, thus making them more proficient in overseeing home studying.

Rewarding a child for good spelling test grades may be done by allowing him to enter a higher spelling group. If he is not quite ready to compete on the next level, the work can be adjusted to his abilities by simply making him responsible for only a percentage of that group's weekly words.

Electric typewriters in a classroom can be a superb reinforcement for spelling. Once the child learns the lower-case letters (touch-typing only), he can use the same words for both spelling and typing practice, thus deriving optimal feedback. (This should be done *only* if teaching touch-typing is a part of the curriculum.)

Science

Science is not one of the subjects that lends itself easily to the creation of instructional sequences. Nevertheless, many aspects of this subject can be sequentialized. If the teacher's thinking has become so oriented, via initial experiences in sequencing the skill subjects (penmanship, arithmetic computations, etc.), certain components in the area of science will become obvious.

First, it is certainly better to consider the use of simple experiements before trying those that are more complex. (It is presumed that the teacher of handicapped learners will not attempt to "teach" science through a text-book-reading method. That is the best way to insure failure!) Experiments should be performed in a single "area" before going on to another. Magnetism or the study of air are fairly good beginning choices. For most of us, who are neither experts in science nor in the teaching of it, a very good source for material is the children's section of the public library. Here, one can find many book titles such as *First Experiments* or *A Child's Book about Magnets and Magnetism*. Look for the easiest ones. These books will help the teacher avoid straying from a discrete behavioral objective. Usually each experiment described is simple, and designed to demonstrate a *single* concept. Once again, this reminder: Practice the experiments at home several times before attempting them in class!

When dealing with children who are not adept at following a series of directions, it is generally advisable for them to observe the teacher doing the experiment before trying it themselves.

An ultimate goal in a science lesson at the higher age and grade levels is for the pupil to be able to explain and/or write up the experiment, listing materials, methods, and probably even drawing a simple diagram to show what happened. The teacher on the earlier levels should keep this in mind and sequence her teachings toward this end. It might enable a pupil who *can* learn and understand science concepts to fit easily into a mainstream science class on the junior high or high school level.

One viable sequential approach might be:

1. At first the teacher will write up the whole experiment, including all diagrams and labels.

2. She will then do all the above except that now the child will do the labeling (providing spelling help and other assistance as needed).

3. Later, the teacher will follow the same procedures as given in "2" except now some gaps are left for the pupil to fill in or a simple question or two about the explanation are interjected.

4. The pupil may then be expected to complete unfinished diagrams as well as labeling them.

The principle here is that, slowly over the year, the requirements are stiffened as the pupil becomes more familiar and more able to function on the higher levels. Note here that the general format for sequential components (such as from teacher guidance to independent work; from smaller to larger volume of work) should be kept in mind.

Teaching science this way, though highly structured, may still be a source of considerable satisfaction for the class and the teacher.

Social Studies

The attitudes one wishes to foster, the broad concepts expected, and the appreciation of other times and cultures one hopes will be nurtured in the pupils through social studies learning are certainly not those in which behavioral objectives are easily stated or brought to fruition. Still, in this area also, sequential thinking can help both teacher and pupil to reach stipulated and measurable goals.

Certain of the social studies concepts are fairly closely related to the more definitive skill subjects. One of these even has the word "skills" in its name. In describing some of the desired goals of learning in geography, the words "map skills" are nearly always included. As the name denotes, they are "skills" which do lend themselves to instructional sequencing. Some of the components should include: from close-at-hand places (e.g., the child's classroom, bedroom, school block, home block, immediate neighborhood, etc.) to places of further distance; from simple road-type maps to product maps, topographic maps, rainfall maps, etc. There are many well-designed atlases and map-skills texts and even kits which can be examined for their sequential properties and utilized by the teacher. Remember, what cannot be purchased in large enough quantities for a class may sometimes be borrowed from materials centers; and ideas may be found in several teaching texts to help the teacher prepare her own materials.

Understanding time lines is a difficult task for handicapped learners; but, when the perspective of their own lives or that of immediate ancestors' lives are the first area of concentration, the earlier era they may be studying can more readily be understood. This is another example of sequence within the area of social studies.

Even more esoteric materials can be altered to meet the pupil's level of comprehension by comparing the new learning to areas in which the pupil is familiar. "Life Styles in Ancient Greece" may be quite nebulous, but a comparison of more discrete and concrete concepts is not. The pupil can explore the ways ancient Greek clothing, farming, or foods were similar to and different from the way we dress, eat, and farm today. The idea generally is to personalize and expand from these very simple concepts to more complex ideas like comparisons of governments and literature, as well as morals and mores. Not all pupils will be able to understand and appreciate all of these concepts; but, if the teacher recognizes the degrees of complexity within the realm of the specific study area, she can individualize and assign to each pupil tasks he can comprehend and in which he can demonstrate what he has learned. She should also utilize simpler materials for learning (pictures, film strips, picture books, etc.) before using more difficult materials like reference books and texts or trade books (i.e., fiction or nonfiction books *not* written as texts).

When planning social studies activities for a self-contained special education class whose members are of diverse ages and grade levels, the teacher is faced with a special dilemma. The children frequently express the desire to learn that which their grade-level peers are studying. This becomes a very sore point, particularly if the teacher gears her selection for study to a "midpoint," in which the entire class (often ranging from grades two to six) will be working on fourth-grade social studies curriculum. There are two possible acceptable solutions—especially if one considers the feelings of the fifth and sixth graders who may legitimately complain that "they studied that twice already!" One answer is individualization. This can be extraordinarily difficult for the teacher (preparation time, finding suitable materials, arranging viable logistics with respect to time blocks and places for learning); and, if individualization is used exclusively, it can deprive pupils of the opportunity to discuss among themselves, as a class, newly-formed ideas and concepts. Another solution—and one generally deemed preferable—is to choose a social studies curriculum less specifically related to that which the grade level might specify, and perhaps treat social studies goals from a different point of view. A study of some of the newer texts can be useful here. Most of them are very careful not to specify grade levels in any way in which pupils can decode them. One example is a series published by the Silver Burdett Co. which approaches the concepts required via a study of man as a social being. They are well highlighted and have many meaningful pictures which are excellent take-off points for discussion; verbiage is cut down; and there are many failure-free questions and success-assured activities.

Social studies is a subject whose outcomes are essentially broad in scope: "to develop an awareness of our American heritage"; " to develop an appreciation of the relationship of geographic factors to economic and social conditions"; "to understand how the weather affects where and how people live"; "to understand the interdependence of all people"; "to realize that America today exists by virtue of the joint efforts of many different peoples throughout past years"; etc. These definitely do not lend themselves to observable behavioral objectives. What is worse, any attempt to reduce social studies to a collection of discrete facts or pieces of knowledge is bound to result in fragmentation, in stereotyping, and in surface memorization of "important" facts (e.g., "Name the capitals of each state." "When did the War of 1812 end?" "Name the immediate and the underlying causes of World War I." "List six products we import from South America.") However, this subject area does involve some specific meaningful skills—using maps and globes, finding information from various sources, using reference materials, developing appropriate vocabulary, etc. These can, of course, be attained through task analysis and instructional sequencing. Even in those aspects of social studies which deal in broad outcomes long-range goals, and the development of social attitudes, the teacher's grasp of—and feeling for—sequencing enables her to plan logical, goal-directed, and smoothly flowing lessons. A broad concept itself, though impervious to sequencing, will be subdivided into a well-organized series of simpler concepts; the lesson parts will all be unified; the pupil will be required to participate actively (i.e., to *do* something); appropriate material will be selected; the pupil's past knowledge (i.e., entering behavior) will be considered; and the teacher will seek to establish some sign by which she can ascertain whether or not the pupil is learning. In a word, she will be teaching rather than presenting.

Sometimes, what seems to be an emotional—rather than an academic—problem can be "treated" by means of instructional sequencing. Suppose that a pupil refuses to write the traditional full heading on any of his school papers, although he is perfectly capable of so doing. By breaking into smaller components the task of heading writing (as if we were dealing with purely an academic deficit), the pupil may thereby be conditioned to perform the behavioral objective. Just as teachers learn to be satisfied with "thimbleful of growth" in slow learners, they must also appreciate "thimbleful of conforming" from pupils who exhibit negativism.

The steps for this sequence could be:

1. The pupil will write only his first name on the top line (left side) of the paper. (In the event that he shares this name with another classmate, his last initial will be included.)

2. Same as Step 1, except now the pupil will also write the date—in number form (e.g., 7/12)—on the top line (right side) of the paper, omitting the year.

3. Increase the requirement to full name.

4. Add the school name (or school number) to the heading directly below the pupil's name.

5. Same as Step 4, except change the date to the written abbreviation (e.g., Oct. 6).

6. Same as Step 5, except add the year to the date.

7. Same as Step 6, except add the class number directly below the date:

John Smith	Oct. 12, 1976
Main Street School	Class 5-3

The teacher's flexibility and her capacity for avoiding thinking in "all or nothing" terms, her skills in translating the overall goal of heading writing into discrete subgoals, and her ability to create modifications (e.g., from writing the month in numbers to writing it with letters)—all prove emotionally supportive. The underlying purpose of this sequence is that it serves as a face-saving strategy.

CHAPTER SEVEN

Parameters of Sequencing

This is the final chapter dealing with *orientation* to the process of creating instructional sequences. Part Two of this book involves the *implementation:* we will put our knowledge of sequencing as discussed thus far to the actual test. Therefore, at this point, it seems judicious to backtrack, to define the broad limits of sequencing, to tie up loose ends. We must clarify what sequences are and what they are not. We must stipulate what they can do and what they cannot do. We must specify when they should be used and when they should not be used. A consideration of the following parameters may help the reader crystallize her thoughts regarding the process of creating instructional sequences, thereby becoming more proficient in it.

A sequence is not necessarily a lesson. Although the time length of a single lesson might be sufficient to cover a given sequence, many sequences will take longer. (This does not mean that a lesson in itself cannot possess a certain unity of its own; whether or not the terminal objective of the sequence has been reached, the lesson itself should have a well-planned beginning, middle, and end.) Also the practitioner, in planning her lesson, must prepare for such items as length of exposure, repetition, emphasis, rewards, modifications, practice, and evaluation. To deal with these, however, while in the initial process of learning to design instructional sequences, siphons one's attention and energies from the task itself.

It is not necessary for the teacher to have a case history of the pupil in order to devise an effective instructional sequence. There is a paradox here: Clearly, the child is the recipient of all of our teaching productivity; yet, by focusing too completely upon him, we may become less able to provide the very intervention—good teaching—that he needs. In other words, too much emphasis upon the child is likely to result in the draining of our attention and concern with the task.

While in the process of learning to create instructional sequences (for a hypothetical pupil), the teacher need only make two stipulations: (1) The pupil is absolutely ready to learn the objective (that is, his entering behavior attests that his past learnings as well as his physical, neurological, emotional, intellectual, and motivational status render him ready to meet the requirements of the task); but (2) he will be unable to learn it if he does not encounter systematic, precise, well-organized teaching.

In the actual classroom, however, it is imperative that the teacher know the child's entering behavior. This information can serve as the basis for decisions she must make regarding modifications, exposure time, type of reinforcement, strategies for nurturing motivation as well as the selection of the instructional task itself. Even so, however, granted only that the pupil's past learnings match the requirements of the task, no further support, structure, modifications, or motivation may be needed—the well-designed instructional sequence may prove sufficient.

Some educational experiences are not meant to "impart knowledge or a skill," but rather to nurture creativity, develop attitudes and appreciations, provide enjoyment, etc. As such, they do not succumb readily to sequencing. In fact, in *learning* to write instructional sequences, it is usually best to begin with skill subjects such as penmanship, phonics, arithmetic computations, etc., or with discrete motor tasks such as catching a ball, or cutting a piece of paper with scissors, inasmuch as the terminal behavior in these instances is absolutely observable.

It must be pointed out, however, that, even in those areas which center upon broad, long-range goals (attitudes, appreciations, values, etc.) rather than upon skills and knowledge, a sense of sequencing can render the teacher more organized, more purposeful, more dedicated to relevancy, more capable of planning well-developed lessons (in social studies, music appreciation, "lessons" in sharing, etc.)—and therefore, more self-confident.

The gifted learner may also benefit from a systems approach. But, being able to learn a great deal intuitively and incidentally, (1) he may not require it so frequently; (2) his sequences may suffice with fewer steps; (3) the scope can be more advanced (e.g., instead of addition of whole numbers, go on to addition of fractions); and (4) the topic can be one of enrichment.

Writing an effective sequence can be a truly creative experience. Originality does not demand open-endedness, nor does it insist upon broad rather than discrete goals. Teaching a pupil (especially a handicapped learner) to differentiate between the *t* and *d* sounds can be as creative and rewarding an experience for the teacher as nurturing another pupil's appreciation of Mozart. The teacher's quest for supportive cues, her choice of sequential components and her decisions regarding how to combine them, her grasp of technical aspects of the task and how to incorporate them into the sequence, her constant awareness of the specific circumscribed instructional goal, and, above all, her sensitivity to the pupil who cannot learn upon mere presentation—certainly these do not contraindicate divergent thinking. In short, writing instructional sequences calls for creativity, but a very special kind:

disciplined creativity.

There is no such thing as "only one correct sequence" for a given objective. After all, any given instructional objective may elicit many (often from about eight to fifteen) sequential components. From among this array, any number (usually, anywhere from four to ten) may be selected. Once selected, each of these sets of components may be introduced or finalized in different orders. Obviously, the number of combinations and permutations is huge. For any given behavioral objective, it is possible to write literally thousands of different but equally effective sequences. (Alas, it is also possible to write millions of inneffective ones!)

Although the major tenet of this book is that teachers should specify precisely what it is they are endeavoring to teach and then proceed in an orderly, step-by-step fashion, no one is suggesting that they spend all their waking hours in writing instructional sequences. Designing them is indeed time-consuming; and it is not recommended that teachers write them for every lesson—or even for most lessons. There are three important considerations here: First, sequences are retrievable, reusable, and (once created) need never be "re-created." Second, if a teacher decides initially to design one a week—and this is an acceptable and a realistic quota for the conscientious teacher—the experience gained in so doing makes each successive sequence easier to prepare. Short-cuts of abbreviation become more apparent. For example, frequently, following the writing of the initial steps (say, Steps 1 through 3), the next step can begin simply as "Same as Step 3, except. . . . " The repetitive practice in writing initial sequences reduces the time needed to produce subsequent ones.

Finally, without necessarily putting a pencil to paper, the teacher begins to "think" a lesson in terms of its sequential steps. To put it differently, the very act of writing original sequences fosters an awareness of—and a commitment to—precision, relevancy, and organization. This awareness and commitment then hones a teaching style consistent with the principles of task analysis. And this teaching style, once evolved, effects the emergence of a master teacher, one who has internalized this philosophy of matching the requirements of the task to the pupil's entering behavior, and who is a true craftsman, whether actively writing the sequence or not. Even criteria for selection of texts and teaching materials become more precisely defined as teachers begin to look for sequential elements in them. Thus, in yet another way, and still without having to write a word, the teacher's newly-formed ability to conceptualize, and to apply, the principles of instructional sequencing renders her even more effective.

Part Two: Implementation

CHAPTER EIGHT

Ordering Elements of Sequential Components

As stated in Chapter Three, on Guidelines, components are the building blocks upon which instructional sequences are constructed. Each component has a "from" and a "to" element (e.g., from simple to more complex; from use of representative materials to use of numbers; from use of cues to fading of these cues; from using available reference material [alphabet line, multiplication tables chart, a model of a letter in penmanship, etc.] to performing by memory; from verbal prompts to more independent functioning).

The reader will recall that in writing a sequence, the teacher herself, when presented with a given behavioral objective, must think of and list the many sequential components which that objective suggests to her. The following exercises are introductory in that the components have already been formulated. They have been developed to give teachers a genuine "flavor" of components by (1) demonstrating some of the possibilities for components suggested by a given behavioral objective, and (2) providing practice in deciding the order of the two elements (i.e., which is the "from" and which is the "to").

As each pair of elements is presented, one should not feel disappointed that the particular component did not occur to her. ("Now why didn't *I* think of that?") The list is not exhaustive, but merely a sampling of the total pool of ideas which exist for that behavioral objective. The point is, though, that *given the two suggested elements for a sequential component*, the teacher is asked to exercise her judgment regarding which order (*a* to *b*, or *b* to *a*) is more supportive to the learner.

In the discussion of the answers, it will be noted that some items are debatable, while others seem clearly unquestionable. Both types of items have been included by design. It is important for teachers to realize that there is "another side of the coin" to some strategies (here is where the teacher's opinions and ideas come in); but, at the same time, they must avoid automatically assigning this state of fluidity to *all* sequential components (here is where the art of teaching comes in).

The Ordering of Elements

Assuming that you would use each of the components listed below, select the element (*a* or *b*) which you think should come *first* in each set.

Riding a two-wheeled bicycle

( ) 1. a) use a girl's bike
         b) use a boy's bike
( ) 2. a) make turns
         b) ride straight
( ) 3. a) let the pupil ride independently
         b) run alongside the bicycle supporting the pupil (from behind) as he rides.
( ) 4. a) run and mount properly
         b) mount by standing on a box
( ) 5. a) ride on hills
         b) ride on level (or only slightly hilly) terrain
( ) 6. a) ride in traffic
         b) ride in safe areas
( ) 7. a) ride on hard-packed earth
         b) ride on cement surface

Sawing a piece of wood

( ) 1. a) pre-groove the wood for the pupil
         b) let him make the initial groove
( ) 2. a) use thin guidelines (e.g., a pencil line or no guidelines)
         b) use thick guidelines (e.g., felt pen with wide nib)
( ) 3. a) use hard wood
         b) use soft wood
( ) 4. a) guide the pupil's hand as he saws
         b) let him saw independently
( ) 5. a) use a smaller saw and a smaller piece of wood
         b) use a regular saw and a correspondingly bigger piece of wood
( ) 6. a) saw wood
         b) saw soap or styrofoam
( ) 7. a) hold the end of the wood (farthest from the vise) for the pupil
         b) don't hold the end of the wood

Increasing reading comprehension

( ) 1. a) read one or two sentences
         b) read several paragraphs

( ) 2. a) ask questions which require making inferences
     b) ask questions which require recall
( ) 3. a) the pupil must retrieve the answer from memory
     b) allow the pupil to refer to the text for answer
( ) 4. a) the pupil reads a paragraph and is questioned
     b) the teacher reads a paragraph to the pupil and he is questioned
( ) 5. a) ask a question after the pupil reads
     b) ask a question before the pupil reads
( ) 6. a) select material which is below the reading level of the child
     b) use material which is on level
( ) 7. a) use general subject matter
     b) use material which is of high interest to the pupil
( ) 8. a) use an order of questions which does not correspond with the sequence of the text
     b) use an order of questions which follows the sequence of the text
( ) 9. a) ask questions, but do not give a choice of answers
     b) ask questions, giving two choices of answers

Adding columns of two-digit numbers with exchange

( ) 1. a) use materials
     b) use algorisms
( ) 2. a) use squared materials (illustrating tens and ones)
     b) use dimes and pennies
( ) 3. a) use numbers in which the first two digits of the *ones* column add to *10* evenly, e.g.,

$$\begin{array}{r} 29 \\ 11 \\ +24 \end{array} \qquad \begin{array}{r} 35 \\ 15 \\ +12 \end{array}$$

     b) use numbers in which they add to a sum greater than 10, e.g.,

$$\begin{array}{r} 19 \\ 27 \\ +18 \end{array} \qquad \begin{array}{r} 26 \\ 37 \\ +19 \end{array}$$

( ) 4. a) add more than two addends
     b) add two addends
( ) 5. a) use a "tens box" above the tens column

$$\begin{array}{r} \square \\ 46 \\ 37 \\ 14 \\ +20 \end{array}$$

     b) write down the "carried" number without using a box

( ) 6. a) Let the teacher finish the example after the pupil adds the ones' columns

     b) let the pupil do the whole example

( ) 7. a) assign five examples, all of which require exchange

     b) assign five examples, some with and some without exchange

( ) 8. a) pupil must add all pairs of partial addends, e.g.,

$$
\left.\begin{array}{r} 47 \\ 35 \\ +16 \end{array}\right] \quad \begin{array}{l} 7 + 5 = 12 \\ 12 + 6 = 18 \end{array}
$$

     b) have an addition matrix chart available.

( ) 9. a) pupil must perform the regrouping of the one's column in writing, e.g.,

$$
\begin{array}{l}
24 = 2 \text{ tens} + 4 \text{ ones} \\
36 = 3 \text{ tens} + 6 \text{ ones} \\
\underline{28 = 2 \text{ tens} + 8 \text{ ones}} \\
88 = 7 \text{ tens} + 18 \text{ ones} = 8 \text{ tens} + 8 \text{ ones}
\end{array}
$$

     b) pupil merely "carries" the proper digit to the tens column

( ) 10. a) Use numbers in which the first two digits of the ones column add up to *10* evenly

     b) use numbers which add only to 7, 8, or 9.

$$
\left.\begin{array}{r} 43 \\ 14 \\ +17 \end{array}\right] \qquad \left.\begin{array}{r} 35 \\ 14 \\ +18 \end{array}\right]
$$

( ) 11. a) use examples in which the sums total 99 or less

     b) use examples in which the sums go into the hundreds

( ) 12. a) label each column "T" for tens and "O" for ones

$$
\begin{array}{r}
\boxed{\text{T}}\boxed{\text{O}} \\
24 \\
36 \\
+19
\end{array}
$$

     b) omit labels

Answers and Explanations

Riding a two-wheeled bicycle

1 (a) The absence of the horizontal bar on the girl's bicycle facilitates mounting and dismounting. Initially, this is a very supportive feature for the pupil who feels he is in danger of falling and wants to get off quickly.

2 (b) It is easier to maintain one's balance while riding straight.

3 (b) The teacher's holding of the bicycle is supportive physically as well as psychologically.

4 (b)   Since mounting properly involves balancing by standing on one pedal and swinging into position while the vehicle is in motion, it is obviously quite difficult. Hence, a modified mount is appropriate at first. The point to remember is that although in actual riding, one must mount prior to riding, it does not have to be *taught* in that order.

5 (b)   Level terrain is best for control, yet slightly hilly (downhill) facilitates build-up to optimal acceleration. Anything more steep, however, would be counterproductive. (Steep uphill would require too much effort, and steep downhill would tend toward excessive, possibly uncontrolled speed.)

6 (b)   Riding in traffic could generate anxiety and/or confusion in the trainee. He may be unprepared to cope with sudden decisions which must be made.

7 (a)   True, hard-packed earth may slow the riding process somewhat (i.e., the friction offered by the cement would tend to give a more efficient ride). Nevertheless, it is our belief that the slight drag of the hard-packed earth is more than compensated for psychologically in that generally there is less of a fear of falling on this surface as compared to cement. DE-BATABLE: Some teachers feel that the smooth ride factor outweighs the psychological support factor. Moreover, because hard-pack is usually a bit gravelly whereas cement usually provides a firm, non-slip surface especially while turning, cement has certain psychological benefits of its own.

Sawing a piece of wood

1 (a)   Making the initial groove is one of the most difficult steps in learning how to saw. Doing this for the pupil in the beginning provides a track for the saw, making it less likely for it to "slip off." In fact, some teachers prefer to enlarge the initial groove to such an extent that just several strokes of the saw would cut the wood in two. (This process of inverse chaining, in which the task is so arranged that the pupil must do the last step first, renders success likely at the very outset, thus fostering positive pupil attitude.) Gradually, the size of the groove can be reduced until, finally, the pupil must make his own.

2 (b)   The initial thicker guideline provides the child with a greater margin for directionality error.

3 (b)   Soft wood offers less resistance.

4 (a)   This is an important aid in that it provides kinesthetic cues (in the beginning, the pupil "feels" how the teacher saws), offers kinesthetic feedback (later, as the teacher relaxes her grasp somewhat and the pupil begins doing the sawing, he can feel her immediate correction at the exact moment of error), and is supportive psychologically.

5 (a)   A smaller saw is easier to control. DEBATABLE: Some teachers feel this may require too much small-muscle coordination.

6 (b)   Soap, or styrofoam, is softer, hence easier. DEBATABLE: Some teachers feel that there is too great a difference between these materials and wood; soap cannot easily be gripped in the vise; and the styrofoam may produce an irritating squeak.

7 (a)   Holding the end of the wood for the pupil makes the sawing experience "steadier." He can concentrate on the sawing, and is not distracted (visually or tactually) by a "flapping" piece of wood.

Increasing reading comprehension

1 (a)   The less that the pupil has to remember initially the better.

2 (b)   Mere recall requires less abstract thinking than making inferences.

3 (b)   Clearly, allowing the pupil to refer to the text for the answer gives him an additional option. (After all, he still can try it from memory if he prefers.)

4 (b)   This is supportive in that it has the pupil become accustomed to the general behavior which will be required of him, namely, attending to what is being read (whether or not he himself is doing the reading) and answering questions based upon it. It is easier in that listening skills antedate reading skills developmentally. Certainly, one is aware that some pupils may have impaired auditory processing abilities, but intact visual perception. They will do better without initially having to listen to the teacher read. In real life this must be dealt with. Learning to write instructional sequences, however, does not require case histories, and it is best to approach the stipulated behavioral objective by considering the general category of "poor reading comprehenders" rather than those who are exceptions to the rule. DEBATABLE: Some teachers feel that having the pupil listen to what is being read instead of doing his own reading is irrelevant to the stipulated aim of increased *reading* comprehension.

5 (b)   This is a supportive step in that it prepares the pupil to comprehend. In a sense, we have asked him to concentrate and to use the reading material as a source of specific information even before he begins reading. Conversely, if he does not know what he will be asked, he may not be as motivated or as able to concentrate.

6 (a)   The easier level facilitates smoother reading. The pupil is more likely to be familiar with the vocabulary and concepts. Since he makes better "contact" with the easier material, he will probably understand it better.

7 (b)   High-interest material is more motivating and therefore more likely to promote greater attention.

8 (b)   Trying to answer a given question by looking it up in the text (or even from memory) is facilitated if there is a corresponding order between questions and answers. In other words, it is easier if that portion of the text which contains the answer to question two comes after that which contains the answer to question one, if the last answer can be found at the bottom of the text, etc. This order of correspondence can be seen as a form of structure and lends additional support when it is most needed (that is, in the beginning).

9 (b)   Giving choices of answers is easier simply because it requires recognition rather than memory: If the child has any "handle" whatsoever on that which he has just read, the presentation of the correct answer as one of the two alternatives serves as a prompt. Instead of having the pupil provide an answer from memory (i.e., from an infinite field), we ask him to choose between a field of only two given choices. Later, the number of multiple-choice items should be increased to three or four, before going on to open-ended questions. This technique of providing multiple choice items is particularly beneficial to those children with language and memory deficits who frequently have the word "on the tip of my tongue" but can't say it.

Adding columns of two-digit numbers with exchange

1 (a)   Using materials (especially "real" things, but also representative materials) goes along with the precept of moving from the concrete to the abstract.

2 (a,b) For the pupil who may have problems with the idea of equality in exchange, the use of dimes and pennies as a modification before the squared materials is introduced may be warranted. Most children have had some experiences with money, "change," and money equivalencies. Hence, it is not only functional, but also motivational and reassuring (i.e., familiar). On the other hand, the squared materials

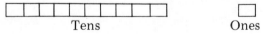

Tens   Ones

are more illustrative of the concept of place value which this behavioral objective requires. (Of course, the pupil should have had previous experiences using squared materials in addition without exchange.)

3 (a)   It is easier to add a number to 10 than to other numbers such as 11, 12, 15, etc.

4 (b)   The numbers are easier (e.g., 4 + 9 is easier than 4 + 3 + 9). Also, the pupil gets to the "carrying" sooner.

5 (a) The "tens box" is a good initial reminder to "carry" properly.

6 (a) The pupil learns through observation. Moreover, it is success-assured, since he should already be familiar with adding one-digit addends. This aspect, if included, must be limited in time. The pupil must fairly soon be encouraged to learn by doing.

7 (a) It is easier at first to avoid having the pupil make the decision regarding whether or not exchange is needed. (Before proceeding to a "mix" of algorisms, exercise in which *only* the decision on whether or not exchange is required [as opposed to working the actual example] should be given.)

8 (b) The matrix chart makes it easier for the pupil who is not sure of his basic addition facts. He does not have to stop to "figure it out."

9 (b) Many pupils, particularly the learning disabled, manifest problems with organization and figure-ground relationships to such an extent that the practice of extending the addends when solving the addition examples is not recommended. Even if the exercise is carefully cued, with lines, color, and adequate spacing, the surfeit of words and activities is overwhelming. The pupil should have had, before this sequence, much experience in extending of numbers without any further steps required. The experience can then be referred to verbally as a cue for the student. DEBATABLE: Some teachers feel that this simultaneous concept-strengthening activity facilitates the mastering of the mechanics of "carrying."

10 (a) For *most* students, adding a number to 10 is easier than recalling combinations of 7, 8, or 9 plus another addend.

11 (a) By dealing with totals which initally do not exceed 99, the pupil does not have to be concerned with the reading and writing of three-place numbers, and with the correct placement of the hundred's digit.

12 (a) The labels remind the pupil which column is the "ones" and which is the "tens," thus preventing confusion.

CHAPTER NINE

Naming Sequential Components

Review the sequential components in the previous exercise. Notice the "crutch factor" of each of the components. They are deemed essential for the handicapped learner. It is this pupil who is absolutely unable to learn the knowledge or skill in question incidentally, tangentially, without systematic, task-relevant, supportive instruction—despite the fact that his entering behavior attests to his overall readiness to engage in that particular learning experience. Thus, sequential components should be regarded as strategic assists enabling handicapped learners to reach a given behavioral objective successfully.

At this point, we should be developing a "mental set" toward identifying sequential components. The key word is *support*. That is, when presented with the stimulus of a stated behavioral objective, the teacher, sensitive to the needs of this hypothetical disabled learner, will immediately identify various sequential components (each stated in the direction of *from* an "easier" element *to* a "harder" element).

When examining the answers to exercises in this chapter, one should bear in mind that each list is not exhaustive. Moreover, additional strategies such as learning to write the numeral 5 by using varied materials (chalk, crayon, fingerpaint, sand, clay, etc.), and by employing an assortment of tracing techniques (completing dotted 5s, going over thickly penciled 5s or 5s which have been cut out of sandpaper, using tracing paper or tracing directly, tracing with finger, pencil, or stylus, "tracing" in the air) will obviously result in an increased number of components.

Theoretically, there is room for considerable differences in choices for answers. Hence, one's answers may be correct and yet not coincide completely with the book's choices. (It should be pointed out, however, that teachers in various workshops and methods courses in which exercises such as these have been presented, generally, for any given instructional objective, come up with a core of identical components with individual variations on only a few of them.)

Naming Sequential Components

List three (or more) sequential components for each of the following instructional objectives. (As mentioned earlier, list them simply in the order in which you think of them. Operational order should not be considered at this point.)

Cutting a piece of paper (8½'' by 11'') into two parts with scissors
  1. from a small piece of paper to a larger piece
  2. from folding paper to not folding paper?
  3. from using verbal clues to no clues

Subtraction of two-digit numbers with exchange
  1. from using materials (e.g., dimes and pennies) to numbers to two digit
  2. from sub. of two digit no. w/o exchange
  3. nos. with exchange x
     from x

Catching a thrown ball (the size of a tennis ball)
  1. from a large ball to a small ball
  2. from a soft ball to a hard ball
  3. from physical assisting to no assistance

Writing the cursive capital letter G on lined paper without the aid of cues or models
  1. from using a model of the letter G to performing by memory.
  2. from physically guiding the hand to no assistance
  3. from verbal cues to no cues

Distinguishing auditorially the m and n sounds, naming and producing either upon command, and identifying either one in a one-syllable word (initial or final position)
  1. auditorially with picture to no pictures
  2. identifying in words orally then in
  3. written words ?
     from initial to final position

78

Naming the letter in the alphabet which goes before or after any given letter
1. from naming the letter that comes after then before.
2. from using a guide,ie,the letters of the alphabet written. to no guide
3. from visual clue ,ie, pointing to the letter A and asking what comes after to no visual clue.

Performing short division with and without remainders having only one-digit numbers for the divisor
1.
2.
3.

Identifying nouns in a series of written sentences
1. from identifying nouns in short sentences to longer sentences.
2. from identifying concrete nouns Then abstract nouns
3.

Distinguishing between simile *and* metaphor
1. from teaching a simile to a metaphor
2. from use of clues such as and like to no clues
3. from oral examples to written examples x

Telling the time correct to the hour and half hour
1. from using a manipulative clock to a regular clock.
2. from hour to half hour
3. from verbal prompts to no prompts x

Following oral multiple orders (up to three consecutive commands)
1. from one to more
2. from simple to complex commands
3. from familar to unfamilar commands

Using a protractor to construct designated angles
1. from starting in the right quar angle to other parts
2. from starting guide to no guide x
3.

Answers and Explanations

For all of the instructional objectives which follow in this section, the components have been numbered only for purposes of identification and references. No hierarchical order is implied.

Cutting a piece of paper (8½" by 11") into two parts with scissors

1. from using a special four-holed scissors (permitting the teacher's physical reinforcement) to regular scissors (These are manufactured commercially. In fact, at least one manufacturer has created a special scissors that fit snugly in the hand. It does not have any holes and it merely requires clenching and opening movements.)

2. from a smaller piece of paper to a larger piece

3. from thick guidelines to thin guidelines

4. from a thin strip of paper (say one-fourth inch) to a wider strip

5. from precutting the paper partially so that just a snip finishes the job to no precutting

6. from the teacher holding one end of the paper taut as pupil cuts (pupil holds the other end) to no teacher support

7. from the teacher giving verbal cues ("close," "open," "stay on the line," etc.) to no cues

8. from using scissors with sharp blades to somewhat duller blades. (This greatly enhances success. There is, of course, the element of danger; precautions, however, can minimize these.)

Subtraction of two-digit numbers with exchange

1. from using real material (e.g., dimes and pennies, weights, postage stamps) to using representative material (e.g., squared material, plastic discs, bundles of tooth picks, Stern's arithmetic rods) to numbers.

2. from the teacher performing the exchange for the pupil (who then finishes the example) to the pupil doing the entire example

3. from drill in determining whether exchange is necessary to no drill (Construct index cards depicting both kinds of examples:

$$\frac{40}{-21} \qquad \frac{65}{-17} \qquad \frac{28}{-11}$$

The pupil inspects the card and tells whether the example requires exchange.)

4. from exchange by expanded notations

$$
\begin{array}{l}
40 = 3 \text{ tens} + 10 \text{ ones}\\
\underline{-29 = 2 \text{ tens} + 9 \text{ ones}}
\end{array}
$$

to exchanging using the traditional shorter notation

$$
\begin{array}{r}
{}^{3}{}^{1}\\
\cancel{4}0\\
\underline{-29}
\end{array}
$$

5. from the teacher providing verbal cues (e.g., "Look at the ones' column. Can you subtract the bottom number from the top number?") to no cues

6. from color cuing (i.e., color the tens green and the ones red) to no color cuing (If this is done consistently at first, the pupil can be instructed to "look at the red numbers only" and determine whether or not the top one is the larger of the two.)

7. from covering the tens' column to no covering (By exposing the ones column only, the decision regarding necessity for regrouping is facilitated.)

8. from making available a chart listing all second decade subtraction facts

$$
\begin{array}{cccccc}
11 & 11 & 11 & & 12 & 12 \\
-2 & -3 & -4 & \cdots & -3 & -4 \\
\hline
9 & 8 & 7 & & 9 & 8
\end{array} \quad \text{etc.}
$$

to memorizing these facts (All cases in which exchange is necessary require the pupil's knowledge of the second-decade subtraction facts. If he is "shaky" in his knowledge of these facts, it may still be advisable to go ahead with the proposed instruction of subtraction with exchange. This can be motivational since he is not held back and he gets additional functional practice in mastering this prerequisite knowledge.)

9. from using a box above the minuend

$$
\begin{array}{|c|c|}
\hline
3 & 11 \\
\hline
\end{array}
$$
$$
\cancel{41}
$$
$$
-29
$$

to no box (This serves as a reminder to consider regrouping and it provides an organized space for rewriting the "new number." Of course, the pupil must be instructed to cross out the "old" one.)

Catching a thrown ball (the size of a tennis ball)

1. from a large ball to small ball

2. from standing close to pupil to moving further away (Some teachers advocate standing so close to pupil initially that you can actually hand him the ball, thus insuring success.)

3. from rolling the ball to the pupil to throwing the ball to him (Although catching a rolled ball requires a somewhat different negotiation than catching a thrown ball, it still requires ocular pursuit and grasping. The predictable path, and the fact that the ball can be rolled slower than it can be thrown, both facilitate success.)

4. from underhand throw to overhand throw

5. from slow throws to faster throws

6. from physical reinforcement (a teacher aide stands behind the pupil and guides his hands through the catch) to no reinforcement

7. from verbal cues to none

8. from using a baseball glove (even for a large ball thrown slowly) to barehand catch.

9. from a striped ball to a solid colored ball (This can prevent the ball from becoming "lost" in the background.)

10. from bouncing the ball to the pupil to throwing the ball to him

11. from throwing the ball directly towards the pupil's chest, thus requiring a minimum of movement to throwing the ball some distance from his chest requiring stretching, running, catching with one hand, etc.

Writing the cursive capital letter G *on lined paper without the aide of cues or models*

1. from a large G to a small one

2. from the teacher physically guiding the pupil's hand to independence

3. from verbal cues (e.g., "Begin just like the cursive 'l'. Now stop and go towards the window. . . ." etc.) to no verbal cues.

4. from having a model of the G exposed to writing G from memory

5. from tracing (going over a previously written G, using tracing paper, connecting dots, etc.) to no tracing

6. from writing in clay (using a stylus) to writing on paper. (This is an additional sensory experience and hence might reinforce learning. Moreover, it slows down the pupil who does things in a driven, impulsive fashion.)

7. from writing segments of the G (sequential segments, perhaps even inverse chaining) to writing the entire letter

8. from "writing" the G in the air to writing on paper

9. from "writing" the G on the desk with the index finger to writing with pencil and paper

10. from using a starting cue (e.g., "x" at the proposed beginning of the G) to no cue for the starting place

Distinguishing auditorially the initial m *and* n *sounds, naming and reproducing either upon command, and identifying either one in a one-syllable word (initial or final position)*

1. from focus upon each letter individually to beginning discrimination activities (This is to make certain the child can recognize and reproduce both the m and the n.)

2. from having available a chart depicting the letter with a key picture (e.g., m-map, n-needle) exposed to no chart

3. from immediate imitation of sound after the teacher makes it to no sound cue given by the teacher

4. from verbal and/or mirror-viewed kinesthetic cues (e.g., placement of tongue) to no such cues

5. from the pupil naming the letter that the sound represents to the pupil producing the sound when the letter is named for him

6. from naming the letter of the single *pure* sound made by the teacher (either *m* or *n*) to naming the letter when *m* or *n* is followed by a nonsense syllable (e.g., *mah* or *nah*) to finally naming the letter when it is the initial consonant in a known one-syllable word

7. from distinguishing pure sound *m* from pure sound *n* to distinguishing them when combined with a given nonsense syllable

8. from the teacher greatly exaggerating sound of *m* or *n* to sounding them normally

9. from recognition of a series of *m*'s and *n*'s when combined with one specific nonsense syllable to recognizing them when given in a series of different one-syllable words (The consistency of at first using the identical "family" [e.g., *ah*] in repetitive trials gets the pupil "set" to attend to the initial sound only.)

10. from using *m* and *n* sounds in initial position of one-syllable words (or nonsense syllables) to using them in final position (This is in consonance with the principle of not requiring the pupil to have to look for too many things at once. At first, he needs massive practice in the initial position only, then in the final position only, and at the last steps of the sequence, interspersed.)

Naming the letter in the alphabet which goes before or after any given letter

1. from instructing and practice in "what letter comes *after* . . ." to what letter comes *before*

2. from instruction and drill using portions of the alphabet to the entire alphabet

3. from having the model (i.e., chart of alphabet or portion of alphabet) exposed to telling what comes *after* and *before* from memory only

4. from the teacher naming a series of letters in alphabetical order (e.g., . . . *h, i, j, k, l, m, n* . . .), stopping suddenly and asking the pupil to tell the next letter to simply naming the single letter and asking the pupil to name the next one (The former strategy creates more of a "mental set" than naming a single letter.)

5. from oral exercises to written exercises

6. from using color-cued arrows pointing in the respective directions of *after* and *before* in conjunction with the the alphabet (or portion of alphabet) chart to no cues

7. from teacher directing pupil to look at the appropriate portion of the chart for finding answers to using chart independently

8. from beginning of alphabet to later parts of alphabet

Performing short division with and without remainders, having only one-

digit numbers for the divisor

1. from using real materials (e.g., pencils or pennies) to using representative materials (e.g., squared materials) to the written algorism alone

2. from using only examples with no remainder to using only examples with remainders to using a mixture of such examples

3. from using examples with one-place dividends (e.g., $4\overline{)8}$) to using two-place dividends ($6\overline{)36}$)

4. from examples requiring knowledge of easier-to-recall tables (e.g., 2, 5, etc.) to more difficult tables (6, 7, 8)

5. from using a tables' chart or matrix as an aid to no aids (Many teachers feel that even if a pupil is not completely sure of division facts, it can enhance his self-esteem and even improve rote memory *functionally* if he is capable of learning the concepts for division examples.)

6. from one example on a page to several (eight or ten) examples on a page

7. from teacher verbally cuing child to recall reciprocal multiplication facts required (4 x 2 = 8, then 8 ÷ 4 = ?) to no verbal cuing

8. from preparing the examples for the pupil to having him do examples written in a math workbook to copying them from a math book or chalkboard onto work paper (Teacher-written examples can be larger and as few or as many as needed; workbook examples are smaller and often more numerous while copying examples is the most difficult.)

9. from using a cue chart which lists the sequential arithmetic processes (1. divide, 2. multiply, 3. subtract: e.g.,

$$
\begin{array}{lll}
4 \text{ - divide} & 4 & 4 \\
3\overline{)14} & 3\overline{)14} & 3\overline{)14} \\
& 12 \text{ - multiply} & \underline{12} \\
& & -2 \text{ - subtract})
\end{array}
$$

to no chart used

10. from practice in *only* locating the correct column for quotient placement (e.g.,

$$
\begin{array}{c}
x \\
3\overline{)12}
\end{array}
$$

to doing the actual algorism (Often it is a good idea for the student to have an intermediate step wherein two copies of the same worksheet are given. On one, he x-marks the placement of the answer and on the second, he does the example. The x-marked paper can be used as a reference.)

11. from using representative pictures under sign, e.g.,

$$
2\,\overline{\left)\begin{array}{l} \text{xxxx} \\ \text{xxxx} \end{array}\right.}
$$

to using algorism with numbers

$$2\overline{)8}$$

12. from cuing the pupil with the reminder ("the remainder must be smaller than the divisor") to having the pupil remember and utilize this cue

13. from special drill in deciding whether or not a remainder is too large to internalizing this concept

Identifying nouns in a series of written sentences

1. from using nouns which are tangible and can be experienced through the senses (e.g., persons, places, or things) to more intangible ones (e.g., character traits, concepts [honesty, rhythm, philosophy, cleverness, idea, etc.])

2. from identifying nouns orally to identifying written nouns (Some pupils having auditory-perceptual deficits may do better with the written mode; in general, however, the spoken format is more supportive than the written one. Moreover, the teacher may wish to provide initial oral cues—intonations, emphasis, expression, etc.)

3. from using written vocabulary below the pupil's reading grade level to using words on grade level

4. from using nouns depicting items which are present to those which must be remembered or imagined

5. from having to select a noun from a two-word sentence (e.g., "Fish swim"; "Play ball") to using longer sentences

6. from using subject matter which is personalized and motivational for the pupil to using more generalized material

7. from providing verbal cues ("Can you see it?" "Can you touch it?" "Can you put the word 'the' in front of it?" "Is it a person, place, or thing?" etc.) to no cues

8. from having available a chart containing the definition and examples of nouns to removal of chart

9. from originally using the terminology "naming word" to using the formal nomenclature "noun" (Until the pupil has grasped the concept of nouns, it may well be supportive to allow him to use this familiar and meaningful label rather than to require him to master simultaneously this new concept and the strange word "noun.")

Distinguishing between simile *and* metaphor

1. from teaching similes to teaching metaphors (The simile is the basis for metaphor. That is, an understanding of simile can facilitate the understanding of metaphor. The converse is not true.)

2. from recognizing similes when compared to simple adjectives (e.g., blue sky vs. as blue as the sky) to recognizing a simile used

in a sentence with no previous adjective cuing (e.g., The night was black as coal.)

3. from short sentences to longer sentences

4. from verbally cuing pupil to look for *clue* words "as" and "like" to no verbal cues at all

5. from recognizing a metaphor that the pupil has observed the teacher creating from a known simile (e.g., "as fast as lightning" to "a boxer's lightning right hook") to recognizing a metaphor without alluding to its referent simile.

6. from using a wall chart giving definitions and simple examples of metaphors and similes to no chart

7. from using subject matter that is well known to the pupil and relatively basic (e.g., color, shapes, simple moods like happy, sad, etc.) to that which is less familiar, though still on his vocabulary level

8. from using written similes and metaphors below the pupil's reading grade level to written similes and metaphors on grade level

Telling time correct to the hour and half hour

1. from telling time to the hour to telling time to the half hour

2. from using large, toy, manipulatable clocks to regular clocks

3. from using significant, "personalized" times (e.g., 12:00 for lunch, 9:30 for gym, etc.) to using other, less significant times

4. from visual cues (e.g., have the actual words "o'clock" printed near the 12 and "half-past" near the six; color the 12 green and the 6 red) to no cues

5. from naming the time orally to writing the time on paper

6. (Prepare two labeled charts of clock faces—one depicting all the possible "o'clock" times and the other all the possible "half-past" times) from asking the pupil to match a given pictured time with one on the charts to stating a specified time and asking the pupil to identify its equivalent (Visual matching is easier than translating a statement into a pictorial representation.)

7. from using the right half of the clock's face to using the entire face (The numbers are "easier." By concentrating on only half of the numbers at first, one can inject more *identical* drill. Most importantly, perhaps, it paves the way to future lessons in which "5 after____," "10 after____," "20 after____," can be approached prior to learning the harder concept of "10 to____," "20 to____," etc.)

8. from having the difference between the size of the big and little hands exaggerated to using hands of normal size

9. from the teacher placing the hands of a toy clock in the correct position demonstrating a specific time to letting the child place them

10. from naming given times on work sheets which depict clock faces with hands in various positions to performing the converse (i.e., drawing in the hands for each given time.)

11. from calling the small hand "the number hand" and the big hand "the o'clock and half-past hand," to using the appropriate "minute hand" and "hour hand" designations (This cue can be supportive, since, initially, the pupil must remember that the small hand points to the spoken *number* whereas the big hand points to the *o'clock* [12] or the *half-past* [6].)

Following oral multiple commands (up to three consecutive commands)

1. from one sentence to more than one

2. from short commands (e.g., "Stand up"; "Clap hands"; etc.) to longer ones

3. from the teacher repeating the commands to no repetition

4. from helping pupils to repeat the commands verbally prior to performance to performing only (This help may be in the form of unison recitation, wherein the unsure pupil will still get his cues from the teacher.)

5. from using cues (e.g., pointing to objects or directions, providing gestures, etc.) to no cues

6. from physically guiding the pupil through the commands to no guidance

7. from using commands which can be executed quickly to those taking more time

8. from using commands concerning actions which the pupil is likely to enjoy (i.e., personalize the context) to using more generalized topics

9. from touching the pupil prior to stating the commands (thus being sure of his attention) to simply stating the commands

10. from using commands which utilize actions and parts of his body only (e.g., "Stand." "Jump twice." "Touch your toes.") to those involving nouns, adjectives, and prepositions (e.g., "Put the red napkin next to the new puzzle.")

11. from giving multiple commands which are logically related to giving unrelated commands.

Using a protractor to measure designated angles

1. from angles of 90° or less to larger angles

2. from angles in the upper right quadrant of the *x-y* axis graph to angles in any quadrant (The factor of not having to rotate the protractor or the paper initially is supportive by virtue of its consistency.)

3. from initially having the *x*-coordinate as the base (stationary) ray while the other ray's counter-clockwise rotation generates

the angle to reversing this concept (Again, the factor of initially using only the x-axis as the base is consistent and therefore supportive.)

4. from pre-drawing rays sufficiently long so that they intersect (rather than "miss") the protractor's numerical markings to shorter lines (requiring pupil's extending them)

5. from angles of 10° only and their multiples to 10° and 5° and multiples to angles of any size (initially 1° - 90°)

6. from color cuing (spot of paint—same color) the vertex of the protractor and the vertex of the angle to no color cuing

7. from color cuing of 10° and 5° (and multiples) markings on the protractor to no color cuing

8. from using a thicker base line to regular width (There is a "trade-off" here. The thicker width, itself, may result in some inadvertent rotation, yet it facilitates the lining up of the protractor.)

9. from using larger protractor (teacher's model) to using one of regular size

10. from the teacher placing the protractor on the base line, to physically guiding the pupil's placement, to independence

11. from verbal cues to no verbal cues

Sequence for Components on page 82

Starting with a pan of clay + a stylus + a model of a A rep to it (above stylus) the teacher guides the children physically + the teacher gives a verbal cue

2. Just like step I but gradually fade away from clay + do in air

3. Just like step I but do on paper

4. Gradually fade out verbal cue

CHAPTER TEN

Evaluating Instructional Sequences

·The reader who has successfully completed the activities in the last two chapters is now ready for learning how to design original sequences. Chapter Eight, "Ordering Elements of Sequential Components," did not ask the reader to come up with one's own sequential components; rather, it required only the evaluation of given paired elements. It thus attempted to nurture the basic prerequisite capacity for conceptualizing the very structure and characteristics of a sequential component. That is, any sequential component (1) contains a "from" and "to" element; (2) proceeds from greater support to less support; (3) is based on broad variables such as distance, time, size, complexity, abstraction, degree of supervision, degree of physical or verbal guidance, availability of associational assists (e.g., cues, models, prompts, visual or auditory reminders, etc.); (4) is clearly relevant to its referent behavioral objective; and (5) may at times—albeit infrequently—be debatable. This ability to conceptualize the gist of sequential components leads the reader directly to Chapter Nine—"Naming Sequential Components." Here, we presented an array of behavioral objectives. One then had to list—in fact, *create*—the many sequential components generated by each of these. The "answer and explanation" section permitted a comparison of the reader's components with those of the authors. (It is likely that many—but not all—of the reader's ideas would be identical with the text's choices. This is in deference to the fact that there is indeed considerable concensus regarding what constitutes good, precise, systematic, relevant, supportive instruction, but that there is also room for some individual opinions which, though not congruent with the overall pool of frequently mentioned components, may nevertheless be equally effective.)

In the exercises that follow, three behavioral objectives will be stated and the sequential components they generate listed. (The first objective will be familiar, having been considered already in Chapter Eight. The latter two will be introduced here for the first time. This progression, itself, may be supportive to the reader by virtue of its sequential approach.) Immediately afterwards, for each of the behavioral objectives, three instructional sequences based upon these components will be presented. Two of them represent correct answers and the other, incorrect. The two valid sequences will have combined the sequential components in accordance with the format established in Chapter Four. (The reader may wish to review that chapter before proceeding.) As mentioned in Chapter Four, there are three acceptable strategies for combining sequential components:

1. Put them *all* together in the first step; then begin bringing each to completion, one (or sometimes, two) at a time.

2. Put *most* of them in the first step; then begin bringing them to completion, but insert the other(s) at some intermediate step. Continue finalizing.

3. Put a *sequence within a sequence.*

In fact, the reader will have the opportunity not only to tell which two sequences are correct in each set, but to list the particular strategy (number 1, number 2, or number 3) which it illustrates. The inappropriate one will, upon analysis, be seen to have specific categories of shortcomings:

1. It may be in arbitrary or haphazard order.
2. It may move too fast (hence, it will be guilty of *presenting* instead of *teaching*).
3. It may reach the terminal objective midway and yet continue pointlessly.
4. It may, in various ways, be illogical, or may reflect ambiguity.
5. It may violate some of the guidelines previously stipulated.

This incorrect sequence may, however, *appear* valid since, in all but one case, it will be constructed entirely from the list of given sequential components. To avoid being deceived by this semblance of relevance, one should focus upon the key question: Are the sequential components combined in a supportive, logical manner, consistent with the three models established in Chapter Four?

The exercises in this chapter are really two-fold in purpose. First, they test the reader's judgment whether or not sequential components have been combined appropriately, thus honing one's grasp of the three acceptable strategies stated earlier for combining sequential components. Simultaneously, they test—by extension—the reader's evaluation of complete sequences: A value judgment must be made as each sequence is designated appropriate or inappropriate. (This is in contrast to Chapter Eleven, which offers evaluation of only the initial steps of sequences.)

Combining Sequential Components

Rewrite the listing of sequential components on a separate sheet of paper. Then carefully examine the three instructional sequences which follow, comparing each with the list.

Do not expect all components to be included in any one sequence. The list serves as a pool for possible choices. The choice—as indeed the compilation of the original list—is a matter of teacher opinion and preference. Therefore, do not rule a sequence invalid simply because it does not include all of the listed components.

Answer the worksheet at the end of each set.

Sequence I: Reading on Grade Level with Comprehension

Behavioral Objective

When given a story on sixth-grade reading level, the pupil will be able to read it and answer from memory factual and inferential questions concerning it, without any cues.

Entering Behavior

All necessary prerequisites: decoding skills on sixth-grade reading level; appropriate mental age; absence of any significant "reading blocks"; adequate visual abilities and ocular control, language skills, attention skills; etc.

Sequential Components

from reading one or two sentences to longer paragraphs

from reading one paragraph, to several paragraphs, to a page, to a story

from asking questions requiring simple recall to questions requiring inferences

from allowing pupil to refer to the text to retrieving answers from memory

from the teacher reading to the pupil and then questioning him to the pupil reading alone

from asking questions before reading to questioning after reading is completed

from using material below pupil's reading level to using material on level

from using high-interest material to more general topics

from posing questions which follow the order of the text to questions in random order

from multiple-choice questions (beginning with only two choices) to "fill-in" questions to questions requiring the pupil to compose the entire answer

from highlighting (e.g., darker print) the essential facts to no highlighting cues

from asking only one question to increasing the number of questions

from multiple-choice questions in which all incorrect answers are clearly unreasonable to providing several reasonable choices

Instructional Sequence IA

1. The teacher has the pupil select from his sixth grade reader the

story he had liked best. The teacher asks the pupil to tell why he liked it.

2. The teacher asks him questions based upon the first page of the story.

3. The teacher instructs him to read aloud the third page, and asks him three questions about it.

4. The teacher then reads the next page aloud to the pupil. The teacher asks him five multiple-choice questions based on that page.

5. The teacher asks the pupil questions based upon all the pages read thus far.

6. The teacher masks out part of a page, exposing only one brief paragraph, reads it aloud to the pupil, and asks him a question, providing him with two possible choices. Use only factual questions.

7. Same as the preceding step, but inferential questions are now asked.

8. The teacher tells him to finish the story silently and gives him a prepared duplicated question sheet containing a variety of types of questions: multiple-choice, "fill-in," and those requiring the pupil to compose the entire answer.

Instructional Sequence IB

1. The teacher starts with a second-grade reader. The teacher reads a paragraph aloud. Ask the pupil simple recall questions. The pupil looks back to the book if needed.

2. The pupil reads a paragraph silently. The teacher asks him simple recall questions and lets him look back to the book.

3. The pupil reads a paragraph silently. The teacher asks him simple recall questions giving him a choice of answers (e.g., "Was the animal a dog or a cat?"). Do not let him look at the book.

4. The pupil reads a paragraph. The teacher asks him simple recall questions, but does not give him a choice of answers or let him look at the book.

5. The teacher gradually increases the amount of reading to two or three paragraphs and repeats Steps 2, 3, and 4.

6. The teacher increases the amount of reading to a full story, repeating Steps 2, 3, and 4 along the way.

7. As before, but now the teacher asks questions that involve more difficult thinking—such as making inferences.

8. As before, but on a more difficult grade level.

9. The teacher gradually increases to an entire story on the pupil's reading grade level.

Instructional Sequence IC

1. Using a short paragraph on sixth grade level, a topic that is interesting to the pupil, and important facts in darkened print, the teacher asks the pupil to read it and, immediately upon completion, to turn the page over and answer the questions. On the reverse side of the page is a multiple-choice question concerning this paragraph. One answer is obviously correct; all the other choices are grossly unreasonable. (Only factual questions are used in Steps 1 to 5.)

2. Subsequent paragraphs become slightly longer and student finds two to three multiple-choice questions on the reverse side. (Darker print is continued on front for main characters and important facts.)

3. The student progresses to a full page of reading material with six to eight multiple-choice questions. Several of the choices are now reasonable.

4. Use only one short paragraph, lightening the darker print for main characters and ideas. Questions on the reverse side are of the "fill-in" variety. Pupil must provide the correct answers.

5. Paragraphs get progressively longer, and three or four questions appear on the reverse side where the pupil must fill in the blank.

6. A full page of material, with no darkening of main characters or ideas, is read by the student. Eight to ten "fill-in" questions appear on the reverse side of the paper. The teacher gradually introduces questions requiring inference.

7. General reading (as opposed to high-interest) material is presented, one paragraph at a time. Questions on the reverse side of the paper are those that relate directly to the paragraph, but the pupil is given no cue to the answer. Pupil is required to compose an answer. The teacher uses more inferential questions.

8. Reading material progresses to two or three paragraphs; and five or six questions (both factual and inferential) are asked of the pupil where he must compose an original answer.

9. Reading material is a full page in length; and eight to ten questions (both factual and inferential) are presented on the reverse side of the paper.

10. The teacher gradually increases the length to an entire story on the pupil's reading grade level.

Worksheet for Sequence I

For the two that you deem appropriate, write the strategy (for combining the sequential components) that it illustrates: in strategy number 1,
all components are in the first step; in strategy number 2, most components
are in the first step and others are introduced at intermediate steps; in strategy number 3, a sequence within a sequence occurs. For the one that you
judge inappropriate, list the flaws.

Sequence IA is _____ inappropriate _____
                 appropriate or inappropriate

   Strategy illustrated:

      or

   Flaws: haphazard order

Sequence IB is _____ appropriate _____
                 appropriate or inappropriate

   Strategy illustrated: # 2 page 90

      or

   Flaws:

Sequence IC is _____ appropriate _____
                 appropriate or inappropriate

   Strategy illustrated: Sequence within a sequence X

      or   # 1 page 90

   Flaws:

Answers and Explanations for Sequence I

Sequence IA: Inappropriate. Step 1, in itself, is a give-away: Asking the pupil to select a story and to tell why "he likes it best," while perhaps motivating, is essentially extraneous to the stated behavioral objective. Moreover, not one sequential component is contained in this step; therefore, this sequence does not reflect any of the three acceptable strategies for combining sequential components.

Step 2 is ambiguous and illogical. Does the pupil reread the story first? Is he expected to perform from memory? (If he could do this from memory, then, clearly, one is taking him beyond the scope of the behavioral objective.) What kind of questions are asked?

Step 3 requires the pupil to read aloud—but there is no clear purpose for oral reading. Also, asking him three questions is arbitrary, since it is totally unrelated—in number or in type of question—to the preceding steps. One more flaw: Step 2 involved page one, and Step 3 involved page three. Whatever happened to page two?

Step 4 finds the teacher reading aloud to the pupil, but this is generally considered *easier* than the preceding steps' format in which the pupil, himself, did the reading. Asking him five questions seems a logical outgrowth of Step 3's three questions, except that the stipulation of multiple-choice questions here is brought in from left field!

Step 5 seems appropriate. It is a summing up and an assessment step. In reality, it adds nothing to the sequence. It goes virtually without saying that all effective teaching entails such considerations as motivation, repetition, modification, and assessment throughout; therefore, to actually include any of these items in a written sequence is usually unnecessary and may even detract from its appearance, its brisk tempo, its effectiveness. The reason for stipulating assessment at this precise point is not explained within the sequence and is, in fact, arbitrary.

Step 6 introduces three supportive components (masking out of part of a page, using only factual questions, and providing two choices for each answer); but these should have been injected into the sequence much earlier. Moreover, in retrospect, Steps 2, 3, and 5 are vague because they specify neither factual nor inferential questions. Obviously, the questions there would have to be one or the other.

Steps 7 and 8 move along in appropriate fashion, but this is hardly enough to offset all of the prior demerits.

Sequence IB*: Appropriate. This illustrates strategy number 2. Five sequential components are contained in the first step. These include three variables: reading level, length of reading passage, and complexity of questions. The other two components consist of initially (1) letting the teacher read to the pupil and (2) allowing the pupil to refer to the text for verification.

Step 2 completes one of the components: The pupil, rather than the teacher, now does the reading. Step 3 completes another component: the

---

*Sequence IB was designed by Sharon Kramer who graciously gave her consent for its use in this book.

pupil is no longer granted access to the text for assistance in answering, but must perform solely from memory. In this same step, a new sequential component—giving two choices in a multiple-choice question—is introduced. True, this is easier than the condition at Step 1 wherein the teacher merely asked recall questions, without providing any choice of answers. A good case can be made, therefore, for initiating it in Step 1. Saving it for Step 3, however, wherein the pupil, for the first time has to answer without looking back at the book, creates a sense of balance. That is, the cushioning provided by this easier answering format, coming precisely at the moment of increased demands (tension?) can be seen as a psychologically supportive arrangement.

Steps 4 through 9 gradually continue to bring all the components to completion, so that in the final step, the pupil is performing the behavioral objective.

Sequence IC*: Appropriate. This depicts strategy number 1 modified. All of the components are listed in the first step. The variables reflected by these components consist of: (1) length of reading passage, (2) degree of pupil interest the passage generates, (3) degree of darkened print cues, (4) number of questions, (5) complexity of question type, and (6) degree to which it is patently clear what answer choices are correct and what are incorrect. These components are finalized gradually in the succeeding steps. Strategy number 1 is modified here by the decision to go back to only a paragraph in Step 4. This can instantly be seen as supportive, coming at the precise time that the darkened print cues are being faded out and when multiple-choice questions are being replaced with the more difficult "fill-in" variety.

The fact that this sequence began with the sixth-grade level should not mislead anyone into judging it to be inappropriate. The teacher chose to start with the pupil's decoding level while supplying a great deal of support in a variety of other ways.

Sequence II: Copying Three Sentences from Chalkboard

Behavioral Objective

Given three sentences of five to seven words each, on reading grade level, written on the chalkboard (in regular-size writing), the pupil will copy them at his desk without the aid of any cues.

Entering Behavior

The pupil has acquired all the prerequisite skills and knowledge (e.g., can grasp a pencil, knows the letters of the alphabet, can read at a given grade level, etc.). He can copy individual words from the chalkboard.

Sequential Components

from near point (model is at desk) to far point (chalkboard), increasing distance and rotating plane

from copying one sentence to copying three sentences

*Sequence IC was designed by Mildred Seitman who graciously gave her consent for its use in this book.

from copying short sentences to longer sentences

from the teacher boxing in words and spaces for words to providing no boxes

from the pupil starting to copy *at the chalkboard* to gradually rotating plane and copying a board model at seat

from a large chalkboard model to smaller writing

from familiar material to more general material

from the teacher copying first part of sentence with pupil completing it to independent copying

from the teacher reading each word aloud as the pupil copies to the teacher giving no cues.

from underlining (and eliciting from pupil) the "difficult portions" to no prompts

from providing an "x" starting cue on pupil's paper to providing no cue

Instructional Sequence IIA

1. The teacher writes a two-word sentence (familiar material, below grade level) at the top of the pupil's paper, and underlines and discusses "difficult portions." The teacher reads aloud each word as pupil writes.

2. As before, but the teacher increases the length of the sentence and starts using a "tiltboard" to change planes.

3. As before, but the teacher starts generalizing material. Higher grade level.

4. As before, but the teacher increases the distance as well as the tilt. Now the pupil is instructed to write two sentences.

5. As before, but the teacher now writes three *large-sized* sentences on the board, on grade level; generalized material is used.

6. The teacher gradually reduces the size and fades all cues ("difficult portion") and prompts. The teacher does not read aloud.

Instructional Sequence IIB

1. The teacher writes a two-word sentence (familiar material, below grade level) at top of pupil's paper, and underlines and discusses "difficult portions." The teacher reads each word aloud as the pupil, seated, copies.

2. As before, but the teacher increases the length of the sentence and elevates the grade level.

3. As before, but the teacher uses less familiar material and begins fading out prompts ("difficult portions") and cues (teacher reading).

4. As before, but the teacher gradually increases to three sentences, on grade level, generalized material, using no prompts or cues.

5. The teacher repeats Steps 1 to 4, gradually arriving at a 45° tilt

(at the pupil's desk).

6. The teacher repeats Steps 1 to 4, gradually increasing the distance and the tilt, arriving at the full 90° tilt for chalkboard writing (proceeding from a larger to a smaller sample).

Instructional Sequence IIC

1. The teacher writes three sentences on the chalkboard. The teacher then copies two of them on the pupil's paper and asks him to copy the third one himself.

2. The teacher copies one of the sentences and asks the pupil to copy two of them independently.

3. The teacher instructs the pupil to copy all three sentences.

4. The teacher reads each word aloud to the pupil as he copies and also provides pre-drawn boxes on his paper for each word.

5. The teacher gradually fades out these cues as the pupil (seated) continues to copy each sentence.

6. The teacher writes a four-word sentence below his reading grade level on the chalkboard and instructs him to copy it.

7. The teacher gradually increases the length of each sentence, the number of sentences, and the grade level.

Worksheet for Sequence II

For the two that you deem appropriate, write the strategy (for combining the sequential components) that it illustrates: In strategy number 1, all components are in the first step; in strategy number 2, most components are in the first step and others are introduced at intermediate steps; in strategy number 3, a sequence within a sequence occurs. For the one that you judge inappropriate, list the flaws.

Sequence IIA is ___appropriate_____
appropriate or inappropriate

Strategy illustrated: #2 pyp 90   I thought I.

or

Flaws:

Sequence IIB is ___Appropriate_____
appropriate or inappropriate

Strategy illustrated: #2.   I thought I

or

Flaws:

Sequence IIC is ___inappropriate_____
appropriate or inappropriate

Strategy illustrated:

or

Flaws:

Answers and Explanations for Sequence II

Sequence IIA: Appropriate. It illustrates strategy number 2. Most of the components (six of them) are in the first step. The process of bringing these to completion is begun at the very next step. At Step 5, a new sequential component—from large chalkboard model to smaller writing—is introduced. It, and all remaining components, are finalized at Step 6. (As an aside, it should be pointed out that this sequence—and all those deemed appropriate in this section—are in consonance with the guidelines for writing instructional sequences cited in Chapter Three. That is, they do not spend too much time reteaching the prerequisite; they assume motivation; they require the pupil to do something at each step; they teach rather than present, etc.)

Sequence IIB: Appropriate. It illustrates strategy number 3 (also strategy number 2). The paramount sequential component was "from near point (desk) to far point (chalkboard)." Notice how Steps 1 to 4 occur initially at the top of the pupil's paper; they repeat, in toto, at Step 5, still at the pupil's desk, but utilizing a 45° tilt throughout. Finally, they repeat again, but now the model is at the chalkboard, the material to be copied having increased in distance and having been fully established on the vertical plane. (At this point, another component "from larger to smaller sample" was introduced; hence, this sequential arrangement also reflects strategy number 2.)

Sequence IIC: Inappropriate. The pupil actually completes the terminal objective at Step 3. But, if he could truly perform this feat at this point, it would have been a clear case of *presenting* instead of *teaching*. Also, the arrangement here is illogical since the sequence continues. But why continue if the pupil has already mastered the aim? The same situation occurs again at Step 5 (i.e., the pupil reaches the terminal objective before the end, yet the sequence continues).

Many of the components here are obviously out of order. For example, at Step 4, "The teacher reads each word aloud to the pupil as he copies and also produces pre-drawn boxes. . . ." Surely, these were meant to be supportive; but, if so, why were they not introduced earlier before the pupil had to perform the terminal objective unaided? Also, there is some degree of ambiguity. Since Step 6 introduces two variables for the first time—sentence length and reading grade level—a glaring question arises: What should the sentence length and reading grade level be in the *earlier* steps? Certainly, *some* sentence length and reading grade level would have had to be specified as early as Step 1, yet these variables were simply ignored.

A final clue can be seen in Step 1. It simply does not list enough sequential components.

Sequence III: Skimming (a page of a book)

Behavioral Objective

Given a page (on reading grade level) to skim in order to find the answer to a factual question, the pupil, in the absence of any cues or prompts, will be able to comply without having to read every word.

Entering Behavior

Pupil has acquired all the necessary prerequisite skills and knowledge (e.g., decodes and comprehends on a given grade level, has necessary eye muscle control for smooth, rapid skimming, can follow verbal instructions, etc.)

Sequential Components

from a sentence, to a paragraph, to a page

from below reading grade level to on level

from teacher's cue (location on page) to none

from highly differentiated individual paragraphs (by topic and topic sentence) to less differentiated

from rebus to entirely by word

from larger print to regular-size print

from darker print cues highlighting the answer and the surrounding areas to regular print

from a narrower page (three inches) to one of regular width

from answers involving a simple noun or verb to phrases

from instructing pupil to find a specific word to answering a question

from drill (Ask question. Point to various lines—or instruct pupil to stop at given points. Ask him if that portion is related to the question. If so, read carefully, if not, skip.) to no drill.

from one sentence to several *enumerated* unrelated sentences

from highly motivational material to more generalized material

from page with several paragraphs, to page with no paragraphs

Instructional Sequence IIIA

1. The teacher begins with a printed sentence below pupil's reading grade level using large print and motivational topic, and asks pupil to find a specific word. The teacher provides a hint as to proper half (location).

2. Still using large print, a motivational topic, below grade level, the teacher increases gradually to five enumerated, unrelated sentences and continues to provide hints ("first three" or "last three" sentences) for location of given word.

3. As before, but the teacher begins drill exercises (asking pupil to stop and consider whether the word he is seeking is likely to be in that sentence; if not, "skip").

4. The teacher continues drill and location hints, but now uses one paragraph; then uses several paragraphs, no longer enumerated, but highly differentiated by topic and topic sentence.

5. The teacher gradually increases grade level and reduces print size. Instead of finding a given word, the pupil must now answer questions which require a simple noun or verb (the teacher, meanwhile, continuing drill and location hints).

6. The teacher increases the material to a full-length page on grade level. Gradually, the material becomes more general rather than motivational. (Location hints and drill support.)

7. As before, but the teacher now asks questions requiring answers which are phrases or entire sentences. (Paragraphs are no longer highly differentiated by topic and topic sentences.)

8. As before, but the teacher begins gradually to fade out the drill by leading the pupil towards *evaluating as he scans*, whether or not the answer is "close at hand," and taking appropriate action.

9. The teacher uses a page with no paragraphs and instructs the pupil to skim to find the answer. No location cues are provided.

Instructional Sequence IIIB

1. The teacher begins with a page below the reading grade level of the pupil and asks him a question before he reads, telling him to find the answer as quickly as possible.

2. Same as Step 1, but the material gradually increases to reading grade level.

3. Same as Step 2, but now the pupil must find a specific word instead of finding the answer to a question.

4. Using a page below reading grade level, the teacher asks the pupil to find the answer to a question. The print is darkened; the answer and the immediate surrounding areas are highlighted.

5. The teacher now provides only a paragraph, and finally just a sentence (instead of a whole page). The teacher asks him a question before he reads and tells him to find the answer as quickly as possible.

6. The teacher fades out the darkened print cues and introduces rebus cues for the difficult words.

7. The teacher then fades out the rebus cues.

8. The teacher asks the pupil to tell why he likes skimming. She may also teach him other meanings of the word "skim."

Instructional Sequence IIIC

1. The teacher begins with a brief paragraph (25 to 30 words) below the pupil's reading grade level and asks him a factual question. Before he finishes reading it, she asks him to stop and consider whether the answer he is seeking is likely to be "close at hand." If so, she tells him to read carefully; if not, skip. At first, the teacher uses highly motivational text, large print, a narrower page (three inches), and rebus cues.

2. Same as Step 1, but the teacher gradually introduces regular-size print.

3. Same as Step 2, but the teacher gradually increases to several paragraphs and then to a full page (containing several paragraphs).

4. Same as Step 3, but the teacher gradually reaches the pupil's reading grade level.

5. Same as Step 4, but the subject matter becomes more general.

6. Same as Step 5, but the teacher fades out the rebus cues.

7. Same as Step 6, but the teacher increases to regular-size page width.

8. Same as Step 7, but the teacher fades out the "stop-and-think" drill.

9. Same as Step 8, but the teacher gradually uses a page containing no paragraph indentations.

Worksheet for Sequence III

For the two that you deem appropriate, write the strategy (for combining the sequential components) that it illustrates: In strategy number 1, all components are in the first step; in strategy number 2, most components are in the first step and others are introduced at intermediate steps; in strategy number 3, a sequence within a sequence occurs. For the one that you judge inappropriate, list the flaws.

Sequence IIIA is _____ appropriate _____
appropriate or inappropriate

Strategy illustrated:

or

Flaws:

Sequence IIIB is _____ inappriate _____
appropriate or inappropriate

Strategy illustrated:

or

Flaws:

Sequence IIIC is _____ appropriate _____
appropriate or inappropriate

Strategy illustrated:

or

Flaws:

Answers and Explanations for Sequence III

Sequence IIIA: Appropriate. Strategy number 2 is employed. Most of the components (six of them) are contained in the first step. Step 2 completes one of the components, "from one sentence to several enumerated unrelated sentences," and shortly thereafter (in Step 4) two new components which are really outgrowths of the recently-completed one are introduced ("from a sentence to a paragraph to a page," and "from a page with several paragraphs to a page with no paragraphs"). Early in the sequence (at Step 3) a crucial drill exercise was launched and continued throughout until Step 8. Step 9 required the pupil to perform the terminal objective without the aid of any cues. (It should be noted that at no prior step was he expected to do this.)

Sequence IIIB: Inappropriate. A close scrutiny will reveal that at Step 2 the pupil is expected to demonstrate that he has mastered the behavioral objective. But this is absurd, because he has not yet been *taught* anything! There are many steps out of order: Finding a word is *easier* than finding the answer to a question; yet this activity comes at Step 3, after the pupil has already achieved (at Step 2) the more difficult task goal. Similarly, using material which is below the pupil's reading grade level and providing darkened print cues (Step 4), reading a single sentence or a single paragraph (Step 5), and using rebus cues (Step 6) are all supportive strategies provided the pupil moves *from* these *to* the final goal of skimming a page on reading grade level without the aid of cues. But these were given after the pupil had to demonstrate (in Step 2) that he has already mastered the terminal objective. Another illustration of illogic is shown in Step 5: "Now provide him with only a paragraph and finally with just a sentence. . . ." Should not the order here be reversed?

Finally, Step 8 is full of irrelevant, extraneous material. As such, it violates several of the previously stipulated basic guidelines for writing instructional sequences.

Sequence IIIC: Appropriate. This illustrates strategy number 1. All of the selected sequential components appear in the first steps. (There are eight components in all.) They are faded out one by one, so that, at the last step—and only at the last step—the pupil is required to perform the terminal objective unaided.

It was possible to include the "stop and think" drill in the very first step because this sequence began with a paragraph. Sequence IIIA began with a sentence. There, it would not have been advisable to interrupt the pupil in the middle of a single sentence and ask him to decide whether the answer is "close at hand." (After all, the answer would never be far away in a lone sentence.)

CHAPTER ELEVEN

Evaluating Initial Steps of Instructional Sequences

The task of learning to design original sequences of high quality might very well have, as its immediate prerequisite, the ability to evaluate a given sequence. In fact, it should be possible to examine the first steps of a given sequence* and determine whether or not the sequence writer has started out on the right track: The first steps are appropriate if they are in consonance with the guidelines mentioned earlier for writing instructional sequences, and inappropriate if they violate any of them. At this point, it may be helpful for the reader to review Chapter Three, which deals with guidelines. A summary of them follows:

1. Avoid extraneous material.
2. Do not spend too much time in reteaching the prerequisites. (Use what the pupil knows to help him learn the new.)
3. Assume motivation.
4. Identify sequential components.
5. Become proficient in technical aspects of the task.
6. Do not present, teach.
   a. The pupil must *do* something at each step.
   b. Do not expect the pupil to show mastery of the task upon a single teacher demonstration or without *any* instruction at all.

*This skill requires a sharper understanding of the sequencing process than does evaluating an entire sequence. The gestalt of an inappropriate sequence when viewed in toto often has an impact of "wrongness"; whereas an initial step has to be more thoroughly scrutinized.

c. Do not start at too advanced a point.
d. Do not use sequential steps which go beyond the scope of the behavioral objective.
e. Avoid the recipe approach.
f. Do not substitute a variety of instructional activities in lieu of an instructional sequence.

When trying to decide which of the guidelines the first steps of a given sequence may be violating, do not draw from the total listing. An instructional sequence can be poorly conceived, yet the guideline it violates may not be apparent in the first steps. The guidelines which do not readily lend themselves to "first-step inspection" are:

Guideline number 4. Sequential components are the building blocks upon which instructional sequences are made, but many perfectly valid sequences will not list all of them in the initial step. Moreover, in many instances, the very presence of one guideline violation guarantees that number 4 will also be violated. An example of this occurs when the teacher, at the very outset, blatantly orders the pupil to perform the terminal objective without any instruction (guideline number 6b). Clearly, in these cases, no sequential components have been included.

Guideline number 5. Technical aspects of the task (e.g., it is easier to copy at near point if the model is placed directly above—rather than to the side of—the writing paper) are generally not visible until later in the sequence. Moreover, there are many instances of sequences which are rather straightforward and do not have any genuine "technical aspect," per se.

Guideline number 6d. The very phrase "beyond the scope of the behavioral objective" indicates that the sequence writer did not stop upon reaching that stipulated objective, but "went on." Of course, this can only be revealed at the end of the sequence and not in the first steps.

Hence, the pool of possible guideline violations for this exercise consists of numbers 1, 2, 3, and 6a, b, c, e, f. Before pronouncing that a given first step is correct, make sure that you are not deceived by appearances. The sheer presence of support (the inclusion of some sequential components, gradual movements, etc.) and relevance (the activities may be related to the topic one hundred percent) does not in itself insure appropriateness. The yardstick question should be: Are *any* of the guidelines violated?

First steps may be deemed invalid for more than one cause. That is, more than one guideline is violated. For example, a first step which is purely motivational (guideline number 3) may also be considered extraneous (guideline number 1). If a sequence is devoid of any sequential components (guideline number 4), it may well be a "recipe approach" (guideline number 6). Expecting performance without any instruction (guideline number 6b) may be compounded if the pupil is asked to demonstrate mastery—still without instruction—in a variety of ways (guideline number 6f). In such cases, simply list the most pronounced violation (or if you prefer, the overlapping ones as well).

Evaluating First Steps of Instructional Sentences

Write *yes* if you consider the initial steps appropriate; write *no* if inappropriate. (For all *no* choices, indicate the guidelines which they violate.)

Sequence	First One or Two Steps
1. Riding a two-wheeled bicycle	Hold the child's hand as you help him walk a straight line. *no*
2. Sawing a piece of wood	Guide the child's hand as he saws a "pre-grooved" piece of soft wood having a thick guideline drawn on it. *yes*
3. Alphabetizing 10 index cards, each containing a one-syllable word; none of the words will have the same first letter	Teach the child to recognize and to name the letters of the alphabet gradually, stressing one-third of the alphabet at a time.
4. Recognizing auditorially, and to produce upon command, the short-*o* and short-*u* sounds	Keep the key chart—a short-*o* picture (ox) and a short-u picture (umbrella) in view. At first use stimulus words in which the vowel is in the initial position. Say the word, holding the vowel an exagger-*yes* atedly long time as pupil attempts to match the sound he is hearing with the picture.
5. Multiplying by six	Teach the *concept* of multiplication using arrays of twos *no* initially.
6. Differentiating colors	Separate 10 red cubes from 10 blue cubes; then direct the child to do the same.
7. Subtraction of two-digit numbers with exchange (regrouping)	Teach place value, using materials first, then numbers.
8. Understanding (i.e., touching and naming) "top" and "bottom" of a blank sheet of paper placed on a child's desk (i.e., horizontally)	Mount, on the chalkboard, a large picture of a person standing; gradually place the picture on the child's desk. He is instructed to name "top" and "bottom" all along the way.
9. Reading and writing "sentences" utilizing the "more than" and "less than" signs, $>$ $<$, correctly (using numbers 1 to 10)	Teach the child to count from 1 to 10 objects correctly; then have him count 1 to 10 imaginary objects.

10. Solving simultaneous equations (using the basic addition or subtraction method, rather than the substitution method)

$$2x + 3y = 17$$
$$\underline{4x - 3y = \ \ 7}$$
$$6x \qquad = 24$$

$$x = \frac{24}{6} = 4$$

$$2(4) + 3y = 17$$
$$8 + 3y = 17$$
$$3y = \ \ 9, \ y = 3$$

Initially, use equations which are to be added rather than subtracted, in which, at the first step, one of the unknowns acquires the coefficient of zero (thus "disappearing"), in which the remaining two terms have positive rather than negative coefficients, in which division comes out "even," and using "easy" coefficients ranging from 1 to 10.

11. Threading a needle

Invite the neighborhood tailor to address the class.

12. Recognizing auditorially, and to produce upon command, the long-*a* and short-*a* sounds

Give the child a set of pictures, each one demonstrating a long-*a* (e.g., *apron*) or a short-*a* (e.g., *wagon*) word. Tell him to sort them.

13. Making change of a quarter in purchasing single items. (price range: 1¢ to 24¢)

Construct a chart showing that a penny = 1¢, a nickel = 5¢, and a dime = 10¢. Ask him to recite these equivalents, gradually removing the chart.

14. Following multiple commands

Say, "Get the dark green book from the left side of my desk; then skip to the small brown leather chair and put the book under it." Later, have him follow written commands and increase the number of them.

15. Copying from the chalkboard

Write on the chalkboard a paragraph of three or four sentences taken from a text on level with the child's reading ability. Ask him to copy; then write a longer paragraph for him to copy.

16. Dribbling a basketball

Instruct the pupil to crouch slightly and to bounce the ball twice while standing still, providing a verbal cue ("now") at each bounce.

17. Telling time correct to the quarter hour

Teach the child to recognize all the numbers from 1 to 12 and to know their order when in a straight line; later arrange the numbers in a circle.

18. Adding any one-digit number to 9

Using sets of discs (e.g., 9 discs and 6 discs), instruct him to take one disc from the 6 set and to place it in the 9 set, thus making it 10. Then ask him to state the new algorism: i.e., $10 + 5$.

19. Doing the "dead-man's float" (assume that the child is somewhat fearful of water, but that this activity is nevertheless recommended)

Hold the child's hand as he stands in a pool of warm water six inches deep; gradually walk to water twelve inches deep.

20. Doing short division with remainder, e.g.,

$$\begin{array}{r} 2 \ R \ 1 \\ 4\overline{)9} \end{array}$$

Demonstrate four examples (two with remainders, two with no remainders). Then let the child try to do some by himself.

21. Cutting a piece of paper with a scissors

Use special four-holed scissors. Initially, guide the child's hand physically as he cuts across a piece of 2" x 6" paper.

22. Writing the cursive capital G

Guide the child's hand (by holding his hand, thus leading him as he writes) as he traces over a large cursive capital G written previously by the teacher.

23. Finding locations on the map by pinpointing given longitude and latitude grids

Tell the child to locate a specific point on the map (e.g., 50° North and 70° East) and let him explain how he found it.

24. Forming the plural of nouns

Show the child some irregular examples (e.g., sheep, mice, teeth) and ask him to think of others.

25. Subtracting mixed numbers (e.g., 6-3/8 – 4-1/4)

Tell him the meaning of "numerator" and "denominator." Then write the proper fraction and ask him to tell the "story" of a numerator and denominator.

26. Differentiating adjectives from other parts of speech

Initially using adjectives which are below the pupil's reading grade level and which are clearly descriptive from the sensory standpoint (e.g., color, shape, size), instruct him to copy 20 sentences from the blackboard. Tell him to underline every word which describes a noun or a pronoun.

27. Multiplying a two-digit multiplicand by a two-digit multiplier: e.g.,

$$
\begin{array}{r}
47 \\
\times 26 \\
\hline
\end{array}
$$

Tell the pupil to (1) multiply the entire top number by the ones' digit of the bottom number (to carry when necessary and to keep numbers in their proper columns); (2) multiply the entire top number by the tens' digit of the bottom number (explain how important it is to indent the answer one space to the left); and (3) add the partial products.

28. Reading numbers in the millions (up to nine places), e.g., 607,050,360

Explain that in our society numbers are always set off by commas in groups of three, starting from the left. Discuss the fact that the paramount prerequisite is the ability to read a simple three-digit number. Tell the pupil that the first group is the ones, the second is the thousands, and the third is the millions. Point out that we must say *millions* or *thousands* but we do not say *ones*. Remind him that each set must have three digits. Discuss the function of zero as a place holder.

29. Differentiating squares from rectangles	Have the pupil tell which is the square and which is the rectangle as you trace their forms in the air, on his back, on his wrist, etc. Tell him to draw a square and a rectangle on paper, in clay, at the blackboard, etc. Ask him to find examples of squares and rectangles in the classroom (desk tops, floor panels, etc.) and at home.
30. Counting by twos from 1 to 20	At first use even numbers only. Have the number line exposed and every even number darkened. Touch the pupil's shoulder rhythmically as he counts the "two more," encouraging him to *think* of the first count, but to *say* the next one. Count in unison with the pupil initially.

Answers and Explanations

1. No. If the child needs help in walking a straight line, he is not nearly ready to learn to ride a two-wheeled bicycle. Guideline violated: number 2.

2. Yes. This approach seems reasonable and contains several supportive sequential components.

3. No. Although the task of recognizing and naming the alphabet letters is related to the task of alphabetizing, it clearly comes first. If the child must be taught these preliminary skills (and remember we are talking about *handicapped learners*), then he is miles away from being ready to learn alphabetizing. Guideline violated: number 2.

4. Yes. Not only are there supportive sequential components here (e.g., from chart exposed to chart removed), but also, the actual strategy of holding the vowel sound a long time, thus facilitating the matching of auditory and visual stimuli, is provided.

5. No. If the child does not know the concept of multiplication (i.e., that it is a special case of addition, that the "bottom number" tells how many times the "top number" is to be counted, what the multiplication sign means, etc.), then why would the

teacher want to begin with six? Guideline violated: number 2.

6. No. Remember the stipulations. Although the pupil is *ready* to learn the objective, he cannot do so unless his is actually *taught*. By no stretch of the imagination does one demonstration of the task by the teacher constitute teaching. This illustration is a perfect case of presenting instead of teaching. Guideline violated: number 6b.

7. No. The pupil should already know place value. It would have come up in prior lessons involving addition of two-digit numbers with and without exchange (regrouping), and in subtraction of two-digit numbers without exchange. (The sheer presence of the sequential component, from materials to numbers, in no way renders this step appropriate.) Guideline violated: number 2.

8. Yes. This approach starts with "where the child is at" (the vertical plane) and begins moving immediately to the new (the horizontal plane). This is in keeping with guideline number 2. Moreover, the support rendered by the gradual transition—he must name *top* and *bottom* all along the way—reflects an awareness of technical aspects of the task (guideline number 5).

9. No. If he cannot already count from one to ten objects, this objective is too far removed from his entering behavior. Guideline violated: number 2.

10. Yes. The initial choice of this type of equation is highly supportive. It contains strategic sequential components (five of them!) and shows an awareness of the technical aspects of the task.

11. No. Remember, if we are assuming that our hypothetical pupil is absolutely ready to learn the objective, this implies motivational readiness as well. Guideline violated: number 3 (also number 1).

12. No. It has an appearance of appropriateness because the activity is entirely relevant to the behavioral objective. But the pupil has received no instruction in this. This is a clear case of presenting—and presenting at its worst, since there was not even a perfunctory teacher demonstration—instead of teaching. Guideline violated: number 6b.

13. No. The activity is relevant to the behavioral objective. But the flaw is that the scope of the activity is too preliminary. If a handicapped learner has not yet mastered the knowledge of how much each coin is worth, then the behavioral objective of making change of a quarter during purchasing is undoubtedly beyond his readiness stage. Guideline violated: number 2.

14. No. Don't let the apparent gradation of complexity engendered in the last sentence's sequential components fool you. Notwithstanding this, if a handicapped learner cannot follow multiple

commands, clearly this sequence was started at too advanced a point. Guideline violated: number 6c (also number 6b).

15. No. Although it is supportive to proceed from sentences to paragraphs, starting with three to four sentences (instead of perhaps, several words) is far too advanced. This is further aggravated by using initial material *on* reading grade level rather than *below* grade level. Guideline violated: number 6c (also number 6b).

16. Yes. The sequential components are supportive (e.g., crouching reduces the distance between the floor and the pupil's outstretched hand). Later, the pupil may be instructed to bounce the ball while walking and finally while running.

17. No. If the pupil cannot recognize the numerals 1 to 12, he is definitely not ready to learn to tell time—and to the quarter hour no less! Guideline violated: number 2.

18. Yes. This strategy of using what the pupil already knows to help him learn the new demonstrates the teacher's proficiency in technical aspects of the task: Most individuals do indeed master the adding of any one-digit number to ten before they can add it to nine. (Naturally, if a given pupil can do neither, then a different approach will have to be employed, or perhaps the teacher may decide to devise a sequence to teach him how to add one-digit numbers to ten, thus nurturing readiness for the nines.) Also, the use of the sequential components—from materials to numbers (i.e., from concrete to abstract) provides additional support.

19. Yes. The sequential components seen in this first step are: from holding pupil's hand to letting go, from warm to cooler water, from shallow to deeper water, and (implied) from water touching legs to water touching face.

   Some teachers have remarked that they feel these activities are too preliminary (i.e., the pupil should get his face in the water quicker). Others, however, believe that they are too advanced (i.e., at first, let him simply sit by the pool and dangle his fingers in it.) In a way, the very existence of these polar views attests to the appropriateness of the answer as presented inasmuch as a balance has been achieved. (These more extreme points of view may be perfectly justified in given instances; but, in *learning* to write sequences for hypothetical cases as opposed to designing them for the actual pupil, it is best to consider handicapped learners *generally*.)

20. No. One demonstration hardly constitutes instruction. If, as hypothesized throughout, we are dealing with an individual who, though ready to learn a given behavioral objective (short division in this case) is nevertheless a handicapped learner, he must be given precise, systematic, step-by-step instruction. The absence of any sequential component (except "from demonstration to solo

performance") is another clue pointing to the inappropriateness of this step. Once more, this is a case of presenting instead of teaching. Guideline violated: number 6b.

21. Yes. The supportive strategies are obvious. The sequential components are clearly stipulated: from four-holed to regular scissors, from physical guidance to independent cutting, from cutting a thin width (two inches) to cutting a longer line, and (implied) from straight to curved lines.

22. Yes. The sequential components are: from physical guidance to independent writing, from writing a large *G* to a smaller one, from tracing to writing, and (implied) from using a visible model to forming the *G* from memory.

23. No. Do not let the fact that the activities are relevant to the instructional objective mislead you. If the pupil is able to comply with the teacher's command at the first step, he does not need the instruction because he already knows how to find grid locations on the map. Guideline violated: number 6b.

24. No. There are no sequential components to speak of, except "from the teacher showing examples of irregular nouns to the pupil listing his own" (and this is hardly supportive). Above all, it starts at too advanced a point. (That is, regular examples [book-books, hat-hats, etc.] should certainly precede irregular ones.) Guideline violated: number 6c (also number 6b).

25. No. If the pupil is indeed ready to learn how to subtract mixed numbers with unlike denominators, then the concept and function of the numerator and the denominator should already have been well established. This would have been encountered previously in subtraction of mixed numbers with like denominators, in adding of mixed numbers with like and with unlike denominators, in adding and subtracting of fractions (as opposed to mixed numbers), in fractional equivalencies, etc. Guideline violated: number 2.

26. No. The presence of two supportive sequential components is not sufficient to negate the fact that this activity presents rather than teaches. The most glaring shortcoming is that the chore of copying twenty sentences is time-consuming, utterly monotonous, and patently irrelevant. It destroys the briskness of tempo and detracts considerably from the stipulated behavioral objective. After all, is the goal to master *copying* or to master *adjective recognition*? Guideline violated: number 1 (also number 6b).

27. No. Technically, the steps are in perfect order, but there is not one supportive strategy or sequential component anywhere. In other words, there is nothing here which would indicate that the teacher is focusing upon a handicapped learner. Guideline violated: number 6e.

28. No. All of these points are important, but if what is shown here constitutes just the first steps, then, clearly, the entire sequence is moving much too fast. Not even a single sequential component is to be found. The worst offense is that the pupil is not required to *do* anything; he merely listens. Guideline violated: number 6a.

29. No. The activities are all related to the task, but there is nothing sequential about their arrangement. Their order is immaterial. Above all, there is no instruction, just a variety of activities. Guideline violated: number 6f (also numbers 6b and 6c).

30. Yes. There are quality sequential components, cues, and supportive strategies throughout. The strategy of *"thinking* the next number," but *"saying* the one after that"—especially with the number line exposed at first—can be most effective.

CHAPTER TWELVE

Creating Instructional Sequences

All of the preceding chapters in the Implementation section were designed to lead the reader, step by step, to the point of being able to write one's first original instructional sequence. These were training chapters and included as much "give and take" communication between us authors and you the reader as is possible to provide within the limited medium of print: The authors "stated" the problem; the reader "voiced" answers. The authors then "told" the correct answers and "articulated" their explanations; the reader "listened," did some rethinking, and "revoiced" answers, making the necessary corrections.

The present chapter, "Creating Instructional Sequences," is the most difficult—and certainly that is the logical arrangement sequentially—in that the two-way discussion is over. As before, the problems are stated and the teacher must respond, but, at this point, the conversation ends; that is, no "answers and explanations" portion follow. You are literally on your own!

There is, however, still some support rendered by virtue of the order of the exercises: Exercise I presents a complete sequence. It includes the behavioral objective, the entering behavior, a list of sequential components generated by the behavioral objective, and the sequential steps themselves. The reader is not required to do anything here, other than examine it in entirety, perhaps viewing it as a culmination of all the preceding chapters of this book.

Exercise II lists a behavioral objective, entering behavior, the sequential components, but only the first sequential step. The reader must complete the sequence. Exercise III is the same as Exercise II, except that no sequential steps are offered. Instead, the reader (culling from the list of given sequential components) must design the entire sequence. Exercise IV stipulates a behavioral objective and an entering behavior, but lists only two sequential components. The reader must complete the list, and then—based upon that list—construct the total sequence. Exercise V is the same as Exercise IV, except that now the reader must compose both the entire list of sequential components and the entire instructional sequence.

Exercise VI, the final exercise, supplies only the entering behavior. You the teacher must formulate an appropriate behavioral objective, identify its sequential components, and create the entire sequence (not unlike the situation which faces classroom teachers daily).

Hints

The reader may decide to review the preceding chapters before attempting these final exercises. Certainly Chapters Three ("Guidelines") and Four ("How to Combine Sequential Components") must be thoroughly mastered before attempting to create original sequences. After all, appropriate sequences must adhere to these guidelines and are constructed from an array of sequential components.

In addition, the following hints may prove helpful:

All sequential components must be brought to completion. That is, don't list only half of a component. For example, if you use a color cue, fade it out; if you use verbal prompts, discontinue them; if you start below the pupil's reading grade level, end the sequence on grade level.

If a step (or part of a step) is used as review, specify it as such. (This helps the teacher differentiate between review and actual instruction.)

Incorporate a sufficient number of sequential components—usually between five and eight—into the sequence. (If too few are utilized, the sequence will probably not be supportive enough.)

Avoid ambiguity. Colleagues sharing your sequence (and, remember, you yourself will wish to re-use it at some future date) should not have to ask: "Do you mean two-digit numbers or one-digit numbers?" "Is the pupil supposed to do it or is the teacher supposed to do it?" "Is an instruction to be written or stated orally?" etc.

Prepare a sufficient number of steps, avoiding big gaps. A sequence in reading should not proceed from a single paragraph directly to an entire story. (Keeping in mind the concept of "the handicapped learner" will help here.)

Do not overlook important logistics. For example, a sequence involving the filing of 40 index cards, taking into account that there is not enough space on a pupil's desk for spreading them out, might stipulate a lesser number of cards at any one time or the use of a small file box.

Make sure that the sequence is completed. For example, if a behavioral objective stipulates the addition of six two-digit addends, do not stop at four addends.

The steps should be in order. Any given step should be preparatory to the next step.

Avoid gratuitous statements. Although the teacher must be cognizant of the whole child, pupil-teacher interaction, behavior modification techniques, and the like, such statements as "The teacher's attitude is paramount," "If the child is tired, discontinue," or "Reward the pupil consistently," are out of place in the written instructional sequence.

All the sequences in the following exercises deal with skill subjects. This is in deference to the fact that in learning to write instructional sequences, these subjects are easier initially: Subjects like science and social studies do not as readily lend themselves to sequencing. (Even within the skill subjects, there is a hierarchy of difficulty: e.g., math is more difficult than phonics or English usage; perceptual-motor tasks such as catching a ball, using a pair of scissors, or copying from the chalkboard are probably the easiest of all.) It is useful to bear this in mind as you continue to practice writing more and more instructional sequences.

Exercise I

Examine the entire exercise. Observe the interrelationship of the parts. The entering behavior attests that the pupil's readiness matches the requirements of the behavioral objective. The behavioral objective, in turn, generates the list of sequential components. Notice how certain of the sequential components have been selected and are enmeshed in the instructional sequence and that the behavioral objective is reached in the last step.

You are not asked to write anything in this exercise.

Behavioral Objective

Given a sheet of 8½" by 11" paper with lines spaced one-half inch apart, the pupil will write his name in manuscript letters (proper height, size, formation, and spacing) without the use of any visual models or cues.

Entering Behavior

The pupil recognizes and can name all the letters of the alphabet. He can write—in manuscript—some of the letters, though they are not always correct in size, formation, etc. He can use a regular-size pencil, employing the correct pincer grasp with ease.

Sequential Components

As mentioned throughout the text, one should not expect *all* the sequential components to be incorporated into the sequence. Remember: Sequential components are written as quickly as they are conceived. This list is to be used as the *pool* of available components. The sequence writer then selects only those which she wishes to utilize in constructing her sequence.

from using a model (letter and name charts) to no model

from using wide-space primary paper with a dotted center line to regular half-inch lined paper

from the teacher's verbal prompts to no such prompts

from the teacher's guiding the pupil's hand to no physical guidance

from "writing" letters in the air, to "writing" letters with fingertips (index and middle finger) on the desk, to writing on paper

from writing the first letter of his name, to writing the first two letters, the first three letters, and finally his entire name

from tracing with a pencil over a completed letter, and then a dotted letter, to writing the letter without tracing

from providing small dots or x's on his paper in order to indicate the starting place of each letter to no such cues

Instructional Sequence

1. The pupil will be shown a farily large manuscript model of his name. He will read aloud the letters (from left to right) and be told, if necessary, that these letters spell his given name.

2. Another model showing only the initial capital letter will be placed on a tiltboard at his desk. With the teacher guiding him verbally and physically, the child will "write" the letter in the air space above his desk as he names the letter.

3. Same as Step 2, except the pupil will now "write" with his index finger on the desk's surface.

4. A sheet of primary paper will be placed on the pupil's desk. It will have five lightly written and five dotted versions of his first initial printed on it. The teacher will guide the pupil's hand in the correct motor movements as he traces over these letters with his pencil.

5. Same as Step 4, except that the pupil will do the tracing without the teacher's guidance.

6. The pupil will be given another sheet of primary paper, and still using the tiltboard model, will write his first initial five times on the paper. The teacher will continue verbal prompts and physical guidance, and will place a dot on the paper to indicate the correct starting place.

7. Same as Step 6, except the teacher no longer provides physical and verbal cues.

8. The teacher repeats the total sequence with the second letter of the pupil's name.

9. The teacher uses a model showing the first two letters of the name and repeats Steps 4 through 7, but now has the two letters on the paper (e.g., G A and $\therefore$ $\therefore$).

10. The teacher repeats the sequence, adding a letter of the pupil's name each time, until all the letters are learned and written correctly on primary paper.

11. The teacher has the pupil trace over (with a pencil) his whole

name which has been printed twice on half-inch lined paper. (At first, the letters are completely formed but with light strokes. The second sample is made of dotted lines.)

12. The teacher removes the whole name chart and has the pupil write his name on half-inch lined paper from memory, gradually fading out the dot-placement cue.

Exercise II

Read the behavioral objective, entering behavior, and sequential components. Notice that only the first step of the instructional sequence is given. (Hint: Now look back at the list of sequential components and try to recognize those which are included in the first step. Then decide strategically whether you wish to proceed with only those or whether additional components will be injected at some intermediate step.)

You should now be able to complete the sequence.

Behavioral Objective

Given five division algorisms requiring regrouping within the tens, where the algorism consists of a one-digit divisor and a two-digit dividend (e.g., $3\overline{)51}$) having no remainders, the pupil will be able to solve them without the aid of any cues or prompts.

Entering Behavior

The pupil is able to solve division examples in which he uses the known reciprocals of multiplication; e.g.,

$$4 \times 7 = 28, \text{ so } \quad 4\overset{7}{\overline{)28}}$$

without remainders and with remainders, e.g.,

$$4\overset{7\ R\ 1}{\overline{)29}}$$

He can also solve division examples in which the tens and ones divide evenly, requiring no regrouping, e.g.,

$$2\overset{44}{\overline{)88}}$$

He understands the concept of division. He knows the multiplication tables, but makes occasional errors.

Sequential Components

from using squared materials to using the written algorism only

from using dimes and pennies to using the written algorism only

from using large, colorfully written (magic marker) examples on drawing paper to teacher-prepared examples on dittoed sheet (somewhat larger than average in size, about one-half inch.)

from larger-size written numerals (about one-half inch) to regular sized numerals

from using examples in which only *one* ten has to be exchanged to examples requiring exchange of two or more tens

from using only examples with two-digit dividends requiring regrouping to using examples with and without regrouping

from having a multiplication matrix chart for reference to performing from memory

from working with the teacher to find the answers and having the pupil simply record them to completely independent work by the pupil

from having a division "procedural chart" available to performing the procedures from memory

from examples based upon easier multiplication tables (e.g., 2, 4, 5) to the more difficult ones (e.g., 6, 7, 8)

from providing practice drill to determine whether or not a given example requires regrouping to no such drill

from large chalkboard writing by the teacher to regular-size chalkboard writing

from the pupil writing at the chalkboard (with the teacher's coaching) to writing at his desk independently

from the teacher performing the regrouping and writing the first digit of the quotient, and requiring the pupil to finish the example, to the pupil working the entire example

Instructional Sequence

1. The teacher puts the algorism $2\overline{)52}$ on the chalkboard in large-size writing and simultaneously displays it with its squared-material representation. She demonstrates, using squared material, the appropriate way of dividing the tens between herself and the pupil, recording the 2 in the model's quotient,

$$\frac{2}{2\overline{)52}}$$

She performs the regrouping (changing the "extra" ten to ten ones and combining these with the algorism's two ones). The pupil then completes the example.

Continue adding sequential steps until the behavioral objective is reached.

Exercise III

After reading the behavioral objective and entering behavior, consider the sequential components. Decide which of these components you wish to use in the construction of your sequence (and which of the three suggested strategies for combining sequential components outlined in Chapter Four your sequence will follow).

Now, it is possible for you to write *all* of the instructional steps (i.e., the entire sequence).

Behavioral Objective

When given a standard twelve-inch ruler, the pupil will be able to measure line segments and straight edges of objects correct to the inch and half-inch without the aid of any cues or prompts. He will state "a little more than . . ." or "a little less than . . ." when appropriate.

Entering Behavior

The pupil can recognize all the numbers 1 to 12. He understands the meanings of "half" and of "more" and "less," and the concept of measuring. He has the necessary visual, coordination, language, and attention skills.

Sequential Components

from measuring to the inch to measuring to the half inch

from using a special ruler (if necessary, teacher-made) showing only the inch and half inch markings to one showing quarter inch and eighth inch as well

from using line segments (and objects) which measure a designated number of inches or "inches and a half" evenly to using those which are "a little more than . . ." or "a little less than . . ."

from the teacher lining up the ruler on the line segment (or along the edge of the object) to the pupil doing this independently

from providing verbal prompts (e.g., "Remember, the beginning of the ruler must be right next to the beginning of the line") to no such prompts

from using small measurements (say, no more than four inches) to larger measurements (The smaller measurement requires less of an eye sweep.)

from color cuing the ruler's edge (a small dot of light paint at the inch and half inch markings) to no color cues

from using a six-inch ruler to using a twelve-inch ruler

from providing drill in estimating lengths to no such drill

Select and combine sequential components. Use these to create the entire instructional sequence.

Exercise IV

Read the behavioral objective and the entering behavior. Only two sequential components are given. (It should be pointed out here that, as all kindergarten and physical education teachers know, there is a relationship between skipping and hopping. To be precise, skipping is achieved by hopping once on one foot and then upon the other while moving some distance from the starting point.)

You are now able to complete the list of sequential components and then compose the entire instructional sequence.

Behavioral Objective

Upon command, the pupil will be able to skip the length of the classroom without any prompts or assistance from the teacher.

Entering Behavior

The pupil can walk and run. He also can stand on either foot and can hop on either foot (albeit somewhat clumsily).

Sequential Components

1. from practice hopping in place to hopping in a straight line
2. from the teacher holding the pupil's hand as he hops to no physical support

Complete the list of sequential components. Combine the ones you choose to create the entire instructional sequence.

Exercise V

Only the behavioral objective and entering behavior are stated.

You may now write the total array of sequential components which the behavioral objective suggests to you. Then, after deciding which of those you will utilize, proceed to compose the entire sequence.

Behavioral Objective

When given the phonogram *ay* and the six initial consonants: *b*, *d*, *h*, *m*, *p*, and *s*, visually (i.e., a separate card is made for each: $\boxed{ay}$, $\boxed{b}$, $\boxed{d}$, . . . $\boxed{s}$), the pupil will be able to blend each consonant with the *ay* correctly, thus producing the word.

Entering Behavior

The pupil knows the sounds of all the consonants, and can recognize and name all the letters of the alphabet. He does not read by the whole-word approach and does not recognize words like *bay*, *may*, or *say*.

Compose a list of sequential components and write the entire instructional sequence.

Exercise VI

Only the entering behavior is given. This one was deliberately chosen because it is one of those entering behaviors which suggests a specific behavioral objective. (Some do not: Exercise I's entering behavior, describing the pupil's level of penmanship, is relatively open-ended and does not point to one particular behavioral objective.) Consider this entering behavior. Does it not suggest a behavioral objective having something to do with forming plurals of those nouns which require more than the mere addition of an *s*?

Write the behavioral objective. Couch it in terms of "observable" behavior. Then compose your list of sequential components and, based upon this list, design the entire instructional sequence.

Good Luck!

Entering Behavior

The pupil can define the word, "noun," and can recognize nouns whether in print or stated verbally. He knows how to form the plural of regular nouns only (i.e., those which simply require the addition of an *s* to the singular form—*pen-pens*, *street-streets*, etc.). He is at fourth-grade reading level.

Part Three:
Perspectives

CHAPTER THIRTEEN

Perspectives

One creates instructional sequences for the sole purpose of imparting knowledge and skills. This book has devoted itself entirely to the purpose of creating instructional sequences. The reader might reason, therefore, that the authors equate all of education with imparting knowledge and skills. This would be an erroneous assumption.

The term "education," if viewed in totality, implies "living a full life" and preparation for so doing. It almost defies definition. In a real sense, it is doing, feeling, believing, thinking, imagining, remembering, sensing, guessing, searching, finding, discovering, accepting, rejecting, questioning, creating, aspiring, wanting, growing, empathizing, adapting. It concerns original thought, initiative, conceptualizing, attitudes and appreciation, partaking in pleasurable experiences per se, socialization, emotional growth and adjustment, insight—all of this as well as mastery of specific skills and knowledge via the intervention of instruction. Hence, it is not suggested that the teacher endeavor to impart knowledge or a skill every minute of every school day. The point is that, when the time comes (and it comes fairly frequently in the case of handicapped learners) for "explaining," "showing how," "coaching," "demonstrating"—that is, for actually *instructing*—the teacher should be proficient in it.

I—Instructional Sequences and Task Analysis

There are several concepts of task analysis. Surprisingly, not all of them lend themselves *directly* to developing the teacher's skill in sequencing instructional objectives. Each, however, has its *raison d'etre*, and each has its contribution to make in the total educational process. The conscientious teacher, constantly striving to attain a high level of expertise, might benefit considerably by an increased awareness of various models of task analysis, some of which are discussed in the following paragraphs.

One school of task analysis emphasizes the articulation of broad developmental requirements for a given task. Within this framework, the task analysis for riding a two-wheeled bicycle would list such factors as directionality, laterality, balance, spatial orientation, kinesthetic feedback, eye-hand coordination, etc. The task analysis for skimming (i.e., scanning a written passage to locate quickly a given word or idea) would include memory, ocular pursuit, visual discrimination, directionality, etc. The task analysis for far-point copying (copying from a chalkboard) entails visual-motor coordination, spatial orientation (i.e., the ability to transpose from the vertical to the horizontal plane), directionality, and the overall process of converting visual cues into kinesthetic expression. In essence, this framework is *process*—rather than *task*—oriented.

Another concept of task analysis involves the selection of a large curriculum topic and to break it into successive subkills. In the illustration (see Figure 1) the large curriculum area—Language Arts—is divided into a set of specific subskills listed in Level I. Each of these, in turn, is sectioned into a new set of even more specific subskills. These new skills (in Level II) are each further broken down, thereby producing Level III's list of skills. A final division occurs resulting in Level IV—the level containing skills with the highest degree of specificity.

It should be noted that this table is a highly abbreviated form of the entire model. In actuality, each of the nine skills listed in Level I produces its own new list. For purposes of illustration, however, the subdivision of only its first skill, decoding, was shown. Similarly, of the five subskills depicted in Level II, only the first, discrimination, was analyzed into its Level III. And following suit, In Level III, only the first area, auditory, was selected to illustrate the final listing in Level IV.

Still another aspect of task analysis is to stipulate for a given instructional objective, the complete array of skills it entails, including all of its prerequisites. For example, adding a series of two-digit addends with and without exchange would list recognition of numerals 1 to 99, conceptualizing adding as a process of "putting together," directionality (left-right as well as up-down), knowledge of basic addition facts from 1 to 10, etc. Looking up words in a dictionary would entail recognition of the letters of the alphabet, knowledge of the letters in alphabetical order, the ability to read from left to right, the ability to select the first letter of words, knowledge of how to move from the beginning of a book (the dictionary) towards the end, and vice versa, etc.

The classic prototype for task analysis—sequencing of discrete instructional tasks—stipulates four elements: behavioral objective, entering behavior, instructional procedure (i.e., the sequential steps, themselves), and assessment. This is the model of task analysis upon which this book has focused. Behavioral objectives, entering behavior, and assessments were discussed in the orientation section. The major concern, however, has been with instructional procedures; and, throughout, the reader has been provided with the rationale, guidelines, and technical assistance for creating instruc-

Figure 1

Sample of a Task Analysis of Language Arts by the
Instruction Objectives Exchange

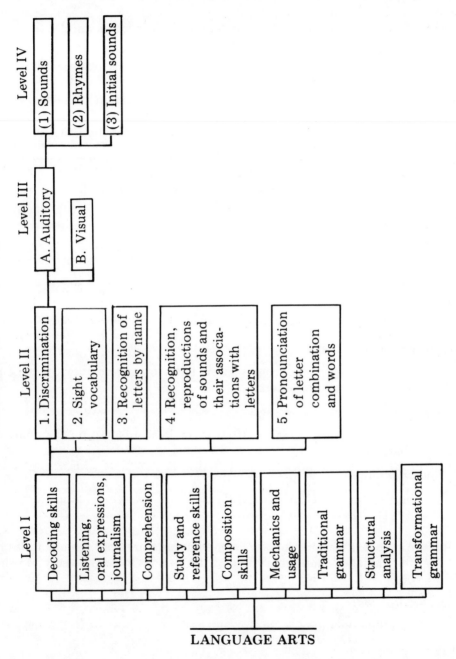

SOURCE: Language Arts Series. The Instructional Objectives Exchange,
Box 24095, Los Angeles, California 90024

tional sequences.

As a result of the preceding descriptions of the four basic models of task analysis, the reader is probably beginning to conceptualize them: their rationale, their style, their differences and similarities. For further clarification, four illustrations follow:

Figure 2a—the broad developmental terms (process) model

Figure 2b—the successive subskills model

Figure 2c—the complete array (including all prerequisite skills) model

Figure 2d—the classic (sequencing of discrete instructional tasks) model

All of them analyze the same behavioral objective: alphabetizing. This facilitates comparisons and cross-references.

Figure 2a
The Broad Developmental Terms (Process) Model

Visual-perceptual skills

visual discrimination (one letter from another); visual sequence (facilitates learning the alphabet in order); visual memory (facilitates memorizing the alphabet)

Auditory-perceptual skills

discrimination, sequence, memory

Figure-ground intactness

e.g., the pupil can locate a given letter on the chart without being sidetracked by the others

Directionality

the ability to look from left to right in words and on the alphabet chart

Spatial orientation

putting one card "in front of," "behind," "between" other cards

Cognitive skills

e.g., classification: letters on index cards are the same as those on the alphabet chart, regardless of differences in size, density of print, etc.

Visual-motor skills

handling the index cards

Additional skills

attention, listening, "order," language

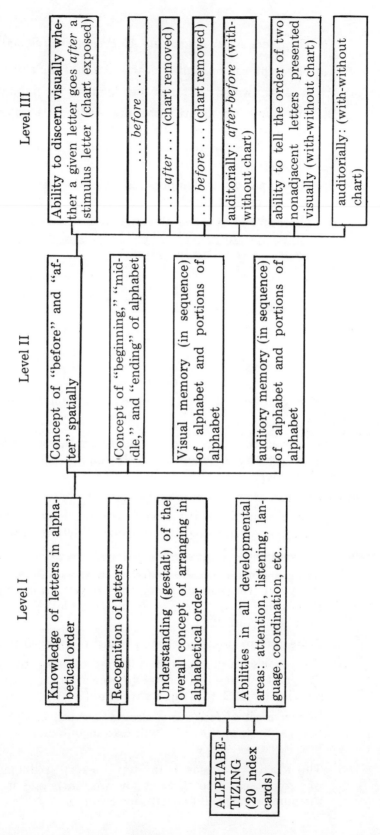

Figure 2b
The Successive Subskills Model

Level I

Knowledge of letters in alphabetical order

Recognition of letters

Understanding (gestalt) of the overall concept of arranging in alphabetical order

Abilities in all developmental areas: attention, listening, language, coordination, etc.

ALPHABE-TIZING (20 index cards)

Level II

Concept of "before" and "after" spatially

Concept of "beginning," "middle," and "ending" of alphabet

Visual memory (in sequence) of alphabet and portions of alphabet

auditory memory (in sequence) of alphabet and portions of alphabet

Level III

Ability to discern visually whether a given letter goes *after* a stimulus letter (chart exposed)

... *before* ...

... *after* ... (chart removed)

... *before* ... (chart removed)

auditorially: *after-before* (with-without chart)

ability to tell the order of two nonadjacent letters presented visually (with-without chart)

auditorially: (with-without chart)

Figure 2c

The Complete Array (Including All Prerequisite Skills) Model

1. The pupil can recognize all the letters of the alphabet (visually).

2. When shown any letter of the alphabet, the pupil can name it.

3. The pupil can identify the first letter of a printed word as opposed to the second, third, or last one.

4. The pupil can match letters on the card with letters on the alphabet chart.

5. The pupil can remember that the first letter of the word—not the others—is the key one.

6. The pupil knows the alphabet in order (roughly) by rote (constant exposure to the "ABC" song and the alphabet chart) but needs to begin with the letter *A*.

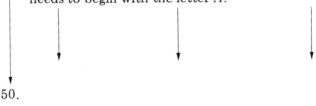

50.

Figure 2d

The Classic (Sequencing Of Discrete Instructional Tasks) Model

Behavioral Objective

When given twenty (3" by 5" index) cards, each containing a word beginning with a different letter, the pupil will arrange them in alphabetical order.

Entering Behavior

The pupil can recite the alphabet from memory (albeit somewhat haltingly) and can name and recognize all letters of the alphabet.

Instructional Sequence

1. Using a portion of the alphabet chart as reference (five letters) the pupil will practice giving the "next" letter after the teacher recites one, two, three, or four of the letters (e.g., "a, b, ___," "a, b, c, ___," or "a, ___")

2. Same as Step 1, except that the chart is removed from view.

3. Shown five cards, each having one of these five letters on it, the pupil will lay out the "next" one after the teacher places any number (from 1 to 4) in a row (e.g., a b ___, or a b c ___).

4. Shown a set of four cards already laid out in alphabetical order (e.g., a, b, d, e) the child will rearrange them to fit the fifth card into its correct place.

5. The teacher proceeds as in Step 4, except reducing the number of prompt cards to three, then two, then one and finally have the pupil arrange all five without prompts.

6. The teacher repeats Steps 3 to 5. using cards with the initial alphabet letter followed by two dashes (e.g., "a — —," "b — —," "c — —," etc.).

7. The teacher repeats Steps 3 to 5, using cards showing three- and four-letter words beginning with *a, b, c, d,* and *e.* (e.g., *ask, bed, come,* etc.).

8. The teacher repeats Steps 1 to 7, with the next five letters of the alphabet *(f, g, h, i, j).*

9. The teacher repeats Steps 1 to 8, but now uses both groups of letters to be used (a→j).

10. The teacher repeats the whole sequence, adding five letters at a time as they follow in the alphabet. This is done until all 26 letters are used to alphabetize twenty word cards.

This book has lead the reader away from all of those educational considerations other than imparting knowledge and skills (see Figure 3). Ours is not a question of which facet of education is the most important. It is simply a matter of treating one specific aspect in detail. The reader is then free—indeed, urged—to back off and view this aspect in perspective, that is, in relationship to the entire educational process.

Similarly, the reader's attention has been directed away from some models of task analysis and towards a specific one. Once there, only one of its four elements has been emphasized. Again, it is fruitless to debate the relative usefulness of each. That they each have considerable merit is incontestable. The "broad developmental terms" concept is a valuable one. It tells the teacher much about the pupil's state of readiness for engaging in a particular learning experience; moreover, if the pupil has a deficit in any of these developmental areas, the teacher cannot help taking this into consideration and dealing with it (via modifications) in her sequence.

The "successive subskills" model can be most useful. First, it tells the teacher to avoid having as an instructional aim such broad statements as "to teach language arts," "to develop arithmetical concepts," "to teach reading," etc. It suggests the necessity for viewing daily lessons against the backdrop of long-range goals. Finally, it can nurture appreciation for—and skill in developing—the overall curriculum.

The "complete array of skills" concept can make the teacher more sensitive to the past learnings which any given instructional objective requires. Thus, while she is in the process of *learning* to create instructional sequences (that is, for the *hypothetical* pupil), it hones her ability to start at the right point. Later, when creating instructional sequences for actual pupils, it renders her astute in regard to selecting goals which are in consonance with the pupil's entering behavior.

The classic model for task analysis is also a useful one. Certainly the teacher must view all the elements in relationship to each other. That the other three elements have considerable import, in themselves, can readily be seen by the emphasis they have received in the past, and continue to receive, in the Education community. Books have been written on the topics of behavioral objectives and assessment. Entering behavior is a vital concern in

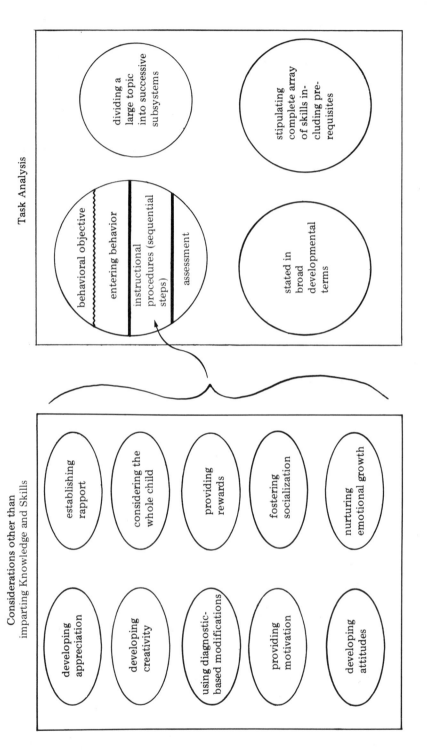

Figure 3

Instructional Sequencing Viewed in Perspective

Considerations other than
imparting Knowledge and Skills

Task Analysis

developing
appreciation

developing
creativity

using diagnostic-
based modifications

providing
motivation

developing
attitudes

establishing
rapport

considering the
whole child

providing
rewards

fostering
socialization

nurturing
emotional growth

dividing a
large topic
into successive
subsystems

stipulating
complete array
of skills in-
cluding pre-
requisites

behavioral objective

entering behavior

instructional
procedures (sequential
steps)

assessment

stated in
broad
developmental
terms

any publication or course devoted to diagnostic-prescriptive teaching. All three are mentioned frequently in texts and courses dealing with behavior modification. By viewing all of these facets and models of task analysis, the teacher is better equipped to see the role of the specific aspect—creating instructional sequences—in the overall educational process. If one had endeavored, however, to discuss all of them simultaneously and with equal valence, the sole topic of "creating instructional sequences" would have been lost in the shuffle. There is an inescapable parallelism here. Just as in designing a sequence, the teacher must concentrate on a single step at a time, this book has focused upon a single aspect of education—creating instructional sequences. This specificity of purpose may be supportive to pupil and teacher alike.

II—Task Orientation and Process Orientation

By definition, children who have been classified as "learning disabled" not only have to be failing in basic skill subjects such as reading, spelling, and arithmetic (despite an average or higher than average IQ), but must also present disorders in one or more broad developmental processes such as language or perception. With the advent of this category (the National Association for Children with Learning Disabilities was founded in 1963) there emerged a growing concern with underlying neurologically processes—and especially with *impairment* in these processes. Indeed, how else was one to explain the phenomenon of individuals exhibiting defective learning skills despite the absence of mental retardation and emotional disturbance? Central nervous system processes (e.g., auditory sequencing, visual discrimination, verbal encoding) were in; emphasis upon the "mere" task, such a thing as copying from a chalkboard, decoding "- *at* family" words, or multiplying by four, was out! It became sophisticated, almost chic, to speak of kinesthetic feedback, tactile discrimination, and spatial orientation; reciprocally, it was rather gauche (and certainly passee) to dwell upon such obvious, surface, and seemingly mundane manifestations like inability to tie shoelaces or to spell correctly. Recently, there has been a trend towards "returning to basics," that is, to deal with those behaviors which the child is emitting, rather than to concentrate on *presumed* underlying causes. This is no picayune argument: If process deficit truly lies at the heart of a child's academic failure, then why spend all our efforts in attempting to remedy *symptoms* when we should be focusing upon the *cause*? On the other hand, if the sole culprit is "simply" the child's inability to master readily certain instructional tasks, then why direct our energies towards correcting some hypothetical, internal, and certainly invisible process that may not even exist?

Stephen C. Larsen has cogently presented the argument, setting forth the major tenets of the *process* method as well as the *task* method (which he calls the *academic* method). The following is a segment of his article published in the *Journal of Learning Disabilities**:

*Stephen C. Larsen, "The Learning Disabilities Specialist: Role and Responsibilities," *Journal of Learning Disabilities* 9:8 (October 1976): 501-503. Copyright © 1976, Professional Press, Inc. Reprinted by special permission of Professional Press, Inc.

Once a child has been identified and labeled as learning disabled, the specialist must plan and conduct an educational program that will enable the child to achieve at a level commensurate with his ability. The nature of the diagnostic and remedial strategies used will be largely determined by the philosophy and professional training of the learning disability specialist. At present there appear to be two basic instructional models commonly employed with the pupil labeled as learning disabled: the process method and the academic method.

The Process Method. Based upon the medical model, the "process" method is predicated on the hypothesis that the majority of these children suffer from some internal disorder that significantly interferes with the efficient utilization (i.e., processing) of sensory data which is derived from the immediate environment. The advocates of this method typically make four basic assumptions regarding the child classified as learning disabled which, to a great extent, dictate the content of their educational intervention. These assumptions include: (1) that children who have learning problems are inherently disabled in some manner (e.g., auditory perception, visual perception, and psycholinguistic disturbances) and therefore are significantly different from "normal" children; (2) that reliable and valid diagnostic instruments are currently available which allow specific identification of the underlying disorder; (3) that once the internal process deficit has been identified, it is amenable to various remedial techniques which will result in generally improved functioning on the part of the child; and (4) that, as a consequence of appropriately applied remediational efforts, performance in listening, thinking, reading, writing, spelling, and arithmetic will be greatly enhanced.

The actual educational procedures utilized by proponents of the process method are to initially administer a battery of tests which are designed to diagnose disturbances in the child's perceptual and/or psycholinguistic functioning. Measures frequently employed for this purpose include the *Marianne Frostig Developmental Test of Visual Perception, Bender Visual-Motor Gestalt Test, Developmental Test of Visual-Motor Integration, Wepman Auditory Discrimination Test, Illinois Test of Psycholinguistic Abilities, Detroit Test of Learning Aptitude, Purdue Perceptual Motor Survey,* and the *Roswell-Chall Auditory Blending Test.* Based upon the obtained results of these tests and other devices, which have usually been administered by someone other than the learning disability specialist, a profile of the pupil's strengths and weaknesses is determined and an educational plan written. At this point, a remedial program is undertaken. It is presumably geared to improve the functioning of the recently diagnosed deficit area(s), to facilitate the continued development of the less severely damaged or normal processing areas, or to do both. Commercial programs commonly used by some specialists include the *MWM Program for Developing Language Abilities* (Minskoff, Wiseman, & Minskoff 1973), *Sound Order Sense* (Semel 1968), the *Frostig Program for the Development of Visual Perception* (Frostig & Horne 1964), and *Aids to Psycholinguistic Teaching* (Bush & Giles 1969). At or near the conclusion of the process training (which may extend from a few months to several years), the remedial program frequently will be expanded to include aspects of direct academic intervention. This phase of training may be conducted by regular classroom teachers, other specialists in the school, or the learning disabilities specialist.

It is obvious that the principles and assumptions underlying process remediation still maintain considerable influence in the field. Indeed, from a historical perspective these procedures as now applied are only slight modifications of those recommended by Goldstein (1939), Strauss (1943), Strauss and Werner (1942), and Strauss and Lehtinen (1947). However, recent research has seriously questioned the effectiveness of this approach when applied to all children who are now designated as learning disabled. In general, these research findings have cast doubt upon whether commonly used process tests actually measure skills that are essential to academic achievement, and whether they possess the necessary power to differentiate between learning disabled and normal children or to accurately predict school success (Cohen 1969, Hammill & Larsen 1974b, Bryan 1974, Larsen & Hammill 1975, Newcomer & Hammill 1975, and Larsen, Rogers, & Sowell 1976). In addition, many of the training programs which are designed to remediate process deficiencies have been shown to be somewhat less than successful (Hammill 1972, Hammill & Wiederholt 1973, Goodman & Hammill 1973, Hammill & Larsen 1974a, and Larsen & Sowell 1975). As a result of these findings and simple disenchantment by some school personnel, this approach seems to be losing popularity in many parts of the country. According to Kirk and Elkins (1974), only 1-16% of the children being seen for instruction in Child Service Demonstration Centers were "... receiving major remedial assistance with processing skills" (p.22).

The Academic Method. The second instructional approach frequently utilized for the child labeled as learning disabled focuses only on those behaviors which have caused the child to be considered somewhat different from his peers. With this method, there is no tacit assumption that the pupil is handicapped by some internal deficit. Rather, if a teacher reports that a child is underachieving in one or more subject areas—e.g., arithmetic, social studies, handwriting, etc.—instructional efforts are directed at diagnosing and reteaching the specific skills and subskills not yet mastered. This does not mean merely tutoring, using the same methods frequently employed in group instruction (which may have been the original cause of the failure). Frequent periods of intensive diagnostic teaching are employed to determine the specific techniques successful with individual children. This method is usually referred to as the "academic" or "behavioral" approach to instruction.

Learning disability specialists who utilize this approach reason: (1) that there is little evidence to indicate that the exact cause of a learning problem can be accurately determined, and even if it were possible, this knowledge would not significantly alter the academically oriented remediation; (2) that the majority of pupils now designated as learning disabled are referred to the specialist for primary academic deficits and any effective teaching strategy must stress the acquisition of those skills and subskills which relate directly to scholastic proficiency; (3) that until the pupil who is labeled learning disabled can adequately listen, read, write, spell, and perform mathematical computations (i.e., to perform satisfactorily in academic subject areas), participation in regular classroom activities will be extremely difficult; (4) that since the vast majority of learning disability specialists are first and foremost trained teachers, their activities should be directed to those areas where they possess demonstrated competency. These teachers prefer not to deal with such multidefined and obscure constructs as "auditory-visual integration," "perceptual-motor," "spatial relations," and "figure-ground," but rather with observable difficulties in consonant blends, addition facts, formulation of capital letters, attention to task, etc.

Since most of the children labeled as learning disabled in the public schools are referred to the learning disability specialist from the regular classroom, advocates of the academic approach usually devote the first portion of their diagnostic process to interviewing the teacher in order to determine specifically why the child is experiencing difficulty in that environment. The interview process is frequently followed by a period of systematic observation in the classroom to validate the teacher's impressions and comments and to ascertain whether the problem is one of true academic retardation, disruptive behavior, poor pupil-teacher relationships, etc. The observational phase is also useful in gauging the possibility of conducting the remediation in that environment.

When necessary, the child is removed from the classroom for periods of diagnosis and remediation. This process involves the administration of various formal and informal assessment devices designed to pinpoint the academic or preacademic skills necessary for the child to achieve at grade level. In every case, the child's responses to specific tasks are carefully monitored and are considered more important educationally than the actual test score. For example, the *KeyMath Diagnostic Arithmetic Test* (Connolly, Natchman & Pritchett 1973) may be administered to a pupil who is having particular problems in mathematical computations. However, discovering that the primary difficulty is in numeration would be more helpful than determining a mere grade equivalent score. Once the particular sequence of skills that have not been mastered has been determined, they are used as the basis of instruction. The specific subskills underlying each major skill are stated in behavioral terms, and this allows a step-by-step presentation of subject matter, and permits efficient evaluation of whether the child has indeed mastered the task. Contingency management systems are frequently employed to encourage maximum performance. As the child progresses through each skill cluster, it is hoped that he or she will gradually approximate grade level functioning. Proponents of this method attempt to facilitate carryover into the regular classroom of remedial work done in relatively isolated situations. It is assumed that until the child is using his newly acquired skills in his normal environment, little real progress has actually been made. The final objective of all remedial efforts is to enable the child to function in the regular classroom as efficiently and effectively as possible.

These two instructional approaches do not operate as precisely as this presentation might indicate. In many cases, efforts are made to combine elements of both methods when planning for the child who is failing in school. However, there is a far greater tendency for proponents of the process method to include aspects of academic remediation than for academically oriented professionals to use components of perceptual and/or psycholinguistic instruction. This observation is supported by Kirk and Elkins (1974) who found that approximately 87% of the diagnosed learning disabled children were receiving primary assistance in the mastery of academic subject areas.

Regardless of which instructional strategies are used by the learning disability specialist, his or her responsibilities are the same. This person must (1) assume major responsibility in organizing and facilitating whatever educational intervention is deemed necessary for the child to perform adequately in school; (2) plan and conduct the diagnostic process where the pupil is either administered a battery of tests or given a short period of intensive diagnostic teaching to determine the areas that require in-depth remediation; (3) carry out, either alone or in conjunction with other professionals, the instructional program that has been designed to bring about improved school performance; and (4) maintain harmonious relationships with regular teachers to insure that the child is adequately supported when in the company of his achieving peers. The manner in which learning disability specialists fulfill these responsibilities will depend on the service delivery system which has been established in the individual school or district.

REFERENCES [Abstracted]

Bryan, T.H.: Learning disabilities: A new stereotype. J. Learning Disabil., 1974, 7, 304-309.

Bush, W.J., and Giles, M.T.: Aids to Psycholinguistic Teaching. Columbus, Ohio: Merrill, 1969.

Cohen, S.A.: Studies in visual perception and reading in disadvantaged children. J. Learning Disabil., 1969, 2, 498-503.

Connolly, A., Natchman, W., and Pritchett, E.: Key Math Diagnostic Arithmetic Test, Circle Pines, Minn.: American Guidance Service, 1973.

Frostig, M., and Horne, D.: The Frostig Program for the Development of Visual Perception. Chicago: Follett, 1964.

Goldstein, K.: The Organism. New York: American Book Co., 1939.

Goodman, L., and Hammill, D.: The effectiveness of the Kephart-Getman activities in developing perceptual-motor and cognition skills. Focus on Exceptional Children, 1973, 4, 1-10.

Hammill, D.: Training visual perceptual processes. J. Learning Disabil., 1972, 5, 552-559.

Hammill, D., and Larsen, S.: The effectiveness of psycholinguistic training. Exceptional Child., 1974, 41, 5-16. (a)

Hammill, D., and Larsen, S.C.: The relationship of selected auditory perceptual skills and reading ability. J. Learning Disabil., 1974, 7, 429-436. (b)

Hammill, D., Wiederholt, J.L.: Review of the Frostig visual perception test and the related training program. In L. Mann, and D. Sabatino (Eds.): The First Review of Special Education, Vol. I. Philadelphia, Pa.: JSE Press, 1973.

Kirk, S., and Elkins, J.: Characteristics of children in resource rooms. Tucson Leadership Training Institute in Learning Disabilities, University of Arizona, unpublished manuscript, 1974.

Larsen, S.C., and Hammill, D.D.: The relationship of selected visual perceptual abilities to school learning. J. Spec. Educ., 1975, 9(3), 281-291.

Larsen, S.C., Rogers, D., and Sowell, V.: The use of selected perceptual tests in differentiating between normal and learning disabled children. J. Learning Disabil., 1976, 9, 85-90.

Larsen, S.C., and Sowell, V.: The effectiveness of the MWM program in developing language abilities. Unpublished manuscript, 1975.

Minskoff, E., Wiseman, D., and Minskoff, J.: The MWM Program for Developing Language Abilities. Ridgefield, N.J.: Educational Performance Associates, 1973.

Newcomer, P., and Hammill, D.: Psycholinguistics in the Schools. Columbus, O.: Charles E. Merrill, 1975.

Semel, E.: *Sound Order Sense. Boston: Teaching Resources*, 1968.

Strauss, A.A.: *Diagnosis and education of the cripple-brained, deficient child. Exceptional Child.*, 1943, 9, 163-168.

Strauss, A.A., and Lehtinen, L.E.: *Psychopathology and Education of the Brain-Injured Child. New York: Grune & Stratton*, 1947.

Strauss, A.A., and Werner, H.: *Disorders of conceptual thinking in the brain-injured child. J. Nerv. Ment. Dis.*, 1942, 96, 153-172.

These two seemingly divergent orientations need not conflict—at least, not totally so. If all parties would concede that these central processes do exist (and this should not be so difficult; after all, we readily assume there is such a "thing" as intelligence, although we cannot see it), then it is possible to stipulate some areas of reconciliation.

It is patently impossible to perform *any* academic task without simultaneously utilizing one or more of the *processes* in question.* When a child writes, he is encoding motorically. When he reads the word *cat*, he is exhibiting visual discrimination. When he recites the numbers one through five upon hearing the teacher do so, he is displaying auditory memory. The implication of this is obvious: When process training is prescribed, it should be implemented; but the *content* of the instruction should be oriented toward academics. Does the child need auditory discrimination training? Fine. Help him learn to differentiate short-*a* words from long-*a* words. Does he require revisualization training? Then give him sequenced practice in looking at his spelling words and remembering them. Is he weak in spatial orientation? Then provide instructional procedures for copying a column of figures.

Even if it were established beyond any doubt that impairment in central processes is the direct cause of underachievement in reading, spelling, writing, and arithmetic, it might still be expeditious to focus treatment upon the symptoms—that is, to offer remediation directly in the subject areas. The field of medicine uses this principle frequently: For example, in many instances of high fever, even those in which the cause is known, the means of treating the cause may be unknown or may require too much time; the common practice is to take immediate steps to reduce the fever. This can't wait. Neither can the school failure!

Creating Instructional Sequences has emphasized task analysis. The sequences presented all smacked of academic tasks. (Some possible exceptions are those dealing with *top* and *bottom*, cutting with scissors, skipping, etc.; but even these can be regarded as task oriented, but at rather elementary academic levels.) The authors focused upon the academic areas since these fall more squarely in the teacher's domain. It should be made clear, however, that sequencing lends itself as readily to process training as to task training. If one wishes to offer instruction designed to remediate figure-background confusion, directionality problems, body image distortion, and other such process impairment, the same educational principles apply:

1. State the behavioral objective based upon the pupil's entering behavior.
2. Formulate a list of sequential components.

*Interestingly, the converse of this is not necessarily true: It is possible to offer perceptual training which is unrelated to academic topics.

3. Following the guidelines for writing instructional sequences stipulated in this book; combine these components into the sequential steps.

In other words, *teach!*

III—Behaviorism and Humanism

Throughout the ages, human beings have been a source of major concern, study, and puzzlement. Scientists, educators, psychologists, anthropologists, historians, as well as religious leaders and philosophers, have sought to unravel the mysteries relating to the development—and intraindividual variations—of thought processes, learning styles, attitudes and values, motivations, coping mechanisms, and other facets comprising the total human being. Since man is so complex, is it any wonder that those who attempt to explain his behavior and to facilitate his learning and/or adjustment often arrive at conflicting conclusions?

Behaviorism and Humanism are two different educational philosophies. Behaviorism holds that man can only be understood by observing and quantifying his behavior, and noting the effects of given variables upon it. Behaviorists deny—or, at least, deemphasize—such considerations as inner thoughts, spiritual growth, and the development of attitude, values, and an esthetic sense, inasmuch as these cannot be measured or observed. They speak of "the brain" rather than "the mind" or "the soul." By behavior, they refer not only to overt actions such as body movement, speech, and facial expression, but also to involuntary functions (e.g., heart beat, pulse rate, brain waves, perspiration, blinking, the reaction of the eye's pupil to bright light), to habits (nail biting, scratching, talkativeness; idiosyncratic sleeping, eating, dressing, and washing routines), and to social interaction (classroom deportment, relationship with peers and family). Learning, itself, is regarded as a behavior—or rather, a behavior modification. And those who endeavor to teach are urged to arrange the conditions for learning (that is to structure the child's instructional environment) in such a way and to provide the necessary psychological reinforcement (either tangible or intangible rewards) so as to enhance the likelihood that learning will occur.

Behaviorists emphasize the role of the teacher: The child learns that which the teacher teaches. They caution us against pronouncing that a given child has learned unless it can be verified. Hence *observable behavioral objectives* are stressed; the desired outcome of a course (or of a lesson) must be stated in terms of what the child is expected to *do* as a result of instruction.

Humanists consider the "whole" child. His affect needs, moral values, and self-concept are paramount. They believe that all learning is not linear—that it can progress in leaps and bounds, at times, *without any teaching;* they point to the joy of sudden discovery—the so-called "Eureka" phenomenon. They stress each child's uniqueness and potential for creativity. They believe that the specified behavioral objective is often not the real purpose of instruction, that *how* the child learns (i.e., his cognitive processes while learning), his understanding, his values, his attitude toward learning are crucial.

This book has focused upon designing instructional sequences; behavioral objectives, therefore, were also emphasized. Hence, one might easily be led to the assumption that the authors promote behaviorism and downgrade humanism. This is not so. To begin with, it has been stated throughout this book that instructional sequences should occupy only a part of the class day; much of the other time can be devoted to those class-room experiences which nurture creativity, values; and attitudes. (Even then, the teacher's knowledge of, and expertise in, sequencing will render her more organized and systematic in arranging these other kinds of experiences. Reciprocally, the effective humanistic teacher, sensitive to the child's emotional, social, personal, and esthetic needs, will cater to each child's uniqueness and will endeavor to make all educational experiences, including the imparting of knowledge and skills, meaningful, fulfilling, and beautiful.)

Granted that the childs self-concept is probably the single most important factor in influencing the attainment of his optimal potential, it might yet be approached through instructional sequencing. In other words, systematic, relevant, organized instruction may succeed in making a learner out of a nonlearner, a winner out of a loser. Despite the fact that this is an indirect approach, it is likely to be more effective than the direct appeal: "Come on, Michael, you're not as bad as you think you are. You should like yourself more."

The fact is that humanism and behaviorism need not conflict. One can instruct by means of behavioral objectives while being totally humane—showing awareness of the emotional needs of the child, relating to him in an acceptant and supportive manner, personalizing the lesson, and of course, by structuring the sequence for success. It is not a question of which is more important, observed behavior *or* cognitive processes. It is simply a matter of the former being the illustrator of the latter.

The humanists' concern with values and attitudes is very justified. All teachers—including those who focus upon observable behavioral objectives—can, by virtue of *their own* values and attitudes, serve as highly visible models.

Humanists often feel that some behaviorists stifle children's creativity and free expression, do not offer them sufficient opportunity to make decisions, and do not let children "do their own thing." However, the handicapped learner unfortunately does not have much of his own "thing" (i.e., a well-defined ego); and many humanists would agree that for him, more teacher intervention and teacher-directed instruction in justified.

What is needed, of course, is the emergence of more and more talented teachers: those who can help the child develop psychologically and socially as well as academically, those who can effectively promote the emergence of values, attitudes and morals, *and* knowledge and skills. The label of the teacher's philosophy is not so important. Certainly, no child should be sacrificed on the shibboleth of a philosophical tenet. The prepotent question should be: *Is it in the child's best interest?* The key, of course, is to provide *quality education.* Just as a master teacher—regardless of which educational ideology she embraces—helps children and facilitates learning, a poor teacher—whether professing humanism or behaviorism—will be ineffective in general, and absolutely disastrous for handicapped learners. Such children are hurt equally by the "humanist" who does not and cannot teach and by the "behaviorist" who is a martinet and is blind to their social, emotional, and personal needs, who literally "trains" rather than teaches. If we can only succeed in combining the best of what humanism has to offer with the best of what behaviorism has to offer, the likelihood that each child we teach will truly fulfill his potential is manifoldly increased!

The Authors

Ernest Siegel, EdD, is among the best known and respected of America's special education professionals. Dr. Siegel received his BA and MA from Queens College (1950, 1951), and his doctorate from Teachers College, Columbia University (1966). He has taught many different kinds of handi-capped children, but has taught regular classes and college-level courses as well. He has published many articles and several books, including *The Exceptional Child Grows Up, Teaching One Child, Special Education in the Regular Classroom*, and *Helping the Brain-Injured Child*. Dr. Siegel is a frequent speaker at conferences and conventions, and has been honored by the Association for Children with Learning Disabilities and the New York Association for Brain-Injured Children. He is presently an Associate Professor of Special Education at Adelphi University.

Rita Siegel, MSEd, received her BA from Queens College (1950) and her graduate degree from Hofstra University (1972). She has taught both regular and special classes in the New York City Schools, where she continues to teach; and she has taught college courses at the University of New Mexico, College of New Rochelle, and Adelphi University, where she currently instructs on a part-time basis. Along with her husband and her son Paul, she is co-author of *Help for the Lonely Child: Strengthening Social Perceptions.*